BARRON'S PARENTING KEYS

KEYS TO INTERFAITH PARENTING

Iris M. Yob, Ed.D.

BARRON'S

DEDICATION

To my parents, who found a way to create a happy interfaith home.

ACKNOWLEDGMENTS

I wish to acknowledge the helpful discussions I had with many people who were willing to share something of their community's practices and beliefs. Among these, I must include Rabbi Sue Shiffron, Sister Mary Montgomery, Reverend Howard Boles, Maha Nourel Din, Sonu Duggal, Shanti Kumar, Janeice Jaffe, Peter Burkholder, Janette Shetter, Pastor Terry Allshouse, Gayle Miles, Dorothy Sowell, Regina Miller, Alan Portzline, Katherine Waggoner, and Phil Vaughn.

All inquiries should be addressed to:
Barron's Educational Series, Inc.
250 Wireless Boulevard
Hauppauge, New York 11788
http: / /www.barronseduc.com

Library of Congress Catalog Card No.: 97-48831

International Standard Book No. 0-7641-0242-7

Library of Congress Cataloging-in-Publication Data
Yob, Iris M.
　　Keys to interfaith parenting / Iris M. Yob.
　　　　p.　　cm.—(Barron's parenting keys)
　　Includes bibliographical references and index.
　　ISBN 0-7641-0242-7
　　　1. Interfaith marriage—United States.　2. Children of interfaith marriage—United States.　3. Parenting—Religious aspects—United States.　I. Title.　II. Series.
　　HQ1031.Y63　　1998
　　649′.1—dc21　　　　　　　　　　　　　　　　　　97-48831
　　　　　　　　　　　　　　　　　　　　　　　　　　　　　CIP

PRINTED IN THE UNITED STATES OF AMERICA
987654321

CONTENTS

INTRODUCTION

W hen two people set up home, they bring together two histories, two extended families, two collections of interests, abilities, and attitudes, two sets of hopes and dreams. That has always been true. No one is a carbon copy of someone else, which is probably a good thing, because life would be dull if we were destined to live with someone just like ourselves. Where would the interest lie? How would we be challenged to rise above ourselves to discover new vistas and conquer distant horizons? How much would we miss out on if we had no "other" to complement ourselves, to confront us with new ideas and novel approaches to life, to learn from, and to come to know and appreciate because they are "other"?

Intuitively we know, however, that not all differences can be blended to create a harmonious family. Some "otherness" repulses us. Some just contradicts us without resolution. Some are like brushing up against a wall of nettles with myriad ways of pricking and scratching. In other words, we cannot live with all kinds of difference no matter how hard we try.

Religious differences have often fallen into this category of irreconcilable differences. Although some couples successfully defy common wisdom, Catholics and Protestants, Jews and Gentiles, easterners and westerners who plan to set up home together are thought by many to be headed inevitably for trouble. And yet, with the expanded mobility of people today and the growing multicultural and multiethnic composition of society, our circle of friends, workmates, and neighbors is likely to be increasingly diverse—and so are our intimate families. More and more people are choosing partners from different ethnic backgrounds, different cultural groupings, different faiths. And many of these families are not only coping with their internal differences, they are thriving on them and making them work for them.

Keys to Interfaith Parenting is written for those who are contemplating setting up home with someone of a different faith or who find themselves already in such a home and are looking for ways to deal with their faith differences, especially in raising their children. At no time does religious diversity have a more profound impact on a family than when decisions have to be made about a child's religious education. Parents, who may have worked out an agreeable arrangement for themselves, are suddenly confronted with a raft of new tensions and conflicts when the baby comes. Why does this happen, and what can be done—for the sake of the parents and the children?

Part One, Exploring the Implications, begins with a look below the surface at what might really be involved when two religions meet. It grapples with questions about what faith is, how interfaith families are composed, what is potentially good and problematic about an interfaith home, and how a couple can prepare to deal with the demands and expectations of their different faiths. Wrestling with these issues can form the foundation for a happy interreligious home.

Part Two, Knowing What to Expect, gives a brief overview of some of the religious traditions around us—Jewish, Christian, Muslim, Hindu, Buddhist—as well as the secularism that characterizes much of the modern world. The purpose of these overviews is to provide some framework for coming to know an unfamiliar faith and especially to indicate in broad terms how that faith is expressed in the home and in the raising of children.

Part Three, Making a Choice, looks at some of the alternatives a couple might consider in deciding on the religious upbringing for their child. It considers the advantages and disadvantages of bringing up the child in the faith of both parents or neither parent or one parent, and how these options can be made to work. It also illustrates some of the general principles that operate across all the options—parenting as teamwork, finding common ground, allowing religious freedom in the home, and dealing with what might be unresolvable dilemmas.

Part Four, Meeting Challenges, takes the view that building a home is a dynamic process and, even with a plan of action already decided, new challenges will emerge. It looks at the kinds of issues that can arise over time in practicing faith in a multifaith home and gives practical suggestions for dealing with them.

Religion is a sensitive subject. Faith shapes people's lives and gives meaning to being human. Religious belief is the source of self-understanding and values. So, when two faiths mix in a home, the couple has serious work to do in planning for their lives together and the raising of their children. If this work is not done, they and their children will likely suffer. If this work is done, the family will be a safe place for children to grow physically, psychologically, and spiritually, and the home will have a positive influence on all who live in it and those who are touched by it. If you, as an interfaith couple, find this book helpful in making your differences work, it will have fulfilled its purpose.

Part One

~~~~~~

EXPLORING THE IMPLICATIONS

Appreciating the implications of an interfaith marriage begins with an understanding of faith itself. Faith is a wide-reaching, self-shaping, value-forming, hope-making combination of belief and trust. Everyone has a measure of faith. What differs is what one has faith in and how one practices that faith.

Because faith involves what one believes, what one does, and what one feels, parents have a great responsibility in building the faith of their children. In a family where the parents have different faiths, exciting challenges as well as potential problems lie ahead. These challenges and problems can best be met when couples prepare for them.

Before embarking on an interfaith marriage, you should ask: Do I understand my own faith and what it means to me? Do I know how my partner's different faith might affect each of us? When you have sorted out your ideas and commitments on a personal level, you have some important planning to do with your partner. What kind of faith do you want to share with your child and how will you go about doing this? Because all families exist in a web of relationships with an extended family and a network of friends, neighbors, and fellow believers, an interfaith couple can prepare these people to respect and support their religious choices. What kind of opposition might you meet from these others and how can you enlist their help in the spiritual development of your children?

The answers to all these questions have lifelong implications. Having the wisdom and courage to address them from the beginning is one of the best preparations a couple can make for their future happiness together and for the well-being of their children.

1

~~~~~~

UNDERSTANDING FAITH

The word "faith" is used in a variety of situations. Someone might say, "I have faith in my car in freezing conditions," and mean that she knows her vehicle is well serviced and will start on a cold morning. Someone else might say, "I have faith that the Hornets will win the finals this year," and mean that his team is playing so well that he can reasonably predict (or hope for) a winning season. Another might say, "I have faith in dreams," and mean that she has confidence that dreams can be trusted when making decisions. And still another might say, "I have got to have faith in my employer," and mean that as the business is downsized he hopes his employer will find him indispensable.

Even in these everyday examples, important features of faith emerge—belief, hope, trust, and confidence. Religious faith also has these same qualities but on a scale large enough to take in the whole sweep of a life, from cradle to grave, through good times and bad. Faith is having something to believe in. Faith is living with hope. Faith is trust. Faith is what makes one confident in the face of an uncertain future. In other words, faith is what one builds a life on.

Faith has been likened to

    an anchor—because it holds a person steady when life gets tempestuous;

a treasure—because it gives rich meaning to life;

a center—because all of life revolves around this hub of beliefs and hopes;

a journey—because it is undertaken throughout a lifetime;

a pathway—because one follows it in all the ups and downs of living;

a map—because it gives a person directions;

a light—because it helps people see things clearly even when their experience is dark;

a life-raft—because it provides a place of certainty and safety in a dangerous world; and

a plant—because it grows when tended.

Faith is also like *a foundation* because it is the basis of peoples' systems of value, helping them sort out the good from the bad, the beautiful from the ugly, and the true from the false. It is the firm ground under their feet when they face a challenge in their life—an illness, a loss, a change of circumstance, or a moment of decision. It shapes their sense of who they are, what their purpose in life is, what their personal responsibilities are, and what their ultimate destiny might be. It underlies how they regard others, the world in which they live, and whatever might be beyond it. It is their bedrock of ideas about the ultimate, or what some would call "God."

When faith is understood in these large terms, it becomes apparent that everybody has a measure of faith, because everybody believes something about the world and about himself, everybody hopes (for something better or worse), everybody trusts something (for good or ill), and everybody is confident about some things. The differences between people are not whether or not they have faith, but what they have faith in and how they practice that faith.

Although faith is a personal quality, many people have a connection of one sort or another to a faith tradition. Religions specialize in faith, for which they maintain organizations, build places of worship, formalize belief systems, cultivate sets of expectations about human behavior and the nature of God (or whatever is considered to be the ultimate), and offer their vision of the good, the true, and the beautiful. The world as we know it today has many different kinds of religions, but these elements are common to most.

While religions remain important, the western world has become increasingly secular. Religion is not as central as it once was in providing people with a faith tradition. The old allegiances to church and God now exist side by side with new allegiances to humanistic values or trust in nature, and to the new authorities of science, nationalism, education, and technology, to name a few. So today, people form their faith from a variety of sources. Living side by side in our communities are people attached to various traditional religious faiths, those with secular commitments, and those who draw their inspiration and faith from a combination of religious and secular ways of knowing, some old and some new.

And sometimes, these people intermarry, bringing into their new homes different ways of understanding and practicing faith. These differences in faith are wide-reaching, since faith itself reaches widely into what one believes, what one hopes for, what one trusts, and what one is confident about. Negotiating these differences, then, especially in the raising of children, is a very significant task for interfaith couples.

2

~~~~~~

FAITH IS A
WAY OF LIFE

E ven when people don't think about their faith all the
time, it is a powerful shaper of who they are. It lies behind their choices and decisions, their commitments
and devotions, their values and moral judgments, and their
hopes and dreams. The life they make for themselves, with its
inspiration and meaning, comes from the faith that they have.
Whatever sources they draw on to build their faith, religious
or secular, it will influence their beliefs, their behavior, and
their inner life of feeling. Faith is a matter of body, mind, and
soul. It is a way of life.

If this seems like an overstatement of the role faith plays
in our lives, here are some things that are influenced by faith.
Faith has an impact on what a person believes, does, and feels.

- *Faith is what a person **believes**.*
  It determines:
  — what someone believes to be the most important thing in
    the world;
  — whether she believes in God and what she believes God
    is like;
  — what she believes about herself—who she is and what
    her purpose in life is;
  — what she thinks about others, beginning with her own
    spouse and children and reaching out beyond the home
    circle to those who are very different from her;

— how she regards the things around her—the natural world, the problems in society, and her responsibility in the community;

— what she thinks is true and what is false and how she knows the difference between them;

— what principles she calls on when she makes an important decision;

— the kinds of things she considers when she is planning her career, her marriage, her family, and her personal growth; and

— the reasons she gives for what she does.

• *Faith is what a person **does**.*

It affects him in:

— what commitments he makes to God, his life's partner, his calling, and his family;

— how he determines his calling;

— what and how he worships;

— the religious observances, duties, or responsibilities he undertakes;

— what he will wear and eat and the kind of house he will live in;

— the kind of volunteer work he will do;

— how he will spend his money;

— what he might choose to do in his leisure time;

— how he will bring up his child and what choices he will make about religious instruction, moral development, discipline, and schooling;

— what the roles of each person in his home will be.

• *Faith is what a person **feels**.*

Apart from determining beliefs and affecting behaviors, faith works deep within the human heart as well. It shapes:

— her sense of the sacred—what she regards as holy, awesome, and ultimate;

— her response to God;

7

— how she worships;
— how she values herself, her family, and others;
— what goals she seeks in life and what priorities she sets;
— what motivates her;
— her prejudices as well as her tolerances;
— her attitudes toward those who seem more fortunate or less fortunate than she;
— whether she lives hopefully or despairingly;
— what she trusts and what she is skeptical about;
— how she shows love, care, and responsibility;
— what she hates and how she deals with it;
— whom she wants to spend her time with and what she wants to spend her energies on; and
— how she faces a crisis.

More can be added to these lists—they simply illustrate how wide the influence of faith is in daily lives. They demonstrate that faith is much more than having one's name on a membership roll or attending services and engaging in occasional rituals. All the externals of faith—belonging to a community and subscribing to a set of beliefs and practices—cannot be isolated from the rest of a person's life. Belief in God or a sense of ultimacy influences everything that person believes. Commitment to a faith, whatever form it takes, shapes all a person's activities and resolutions. Trusting faith gives a pervasive hope and sense of duty to the rest of one's life.

Clearly then, much is involved in an interfaith marriage. Since faith touches on what one believes, what one does, and what one feels, many tensions will need to be resolved for the sake of harmony in the home and for the welfare of any children an interfaith couple may have. There is also the possibility and promise for enriched living for families who enter such a union with good will and the right kind of preparation.

3

‸‸

THE INTERFAITH FAMILY

I f one word can capture the nature of life in the contemporary world, then surely the word "diversity" is a candidate. The world has always been made up of different kinds of people, but today we have come to admit that those differences exist and to make room for them in our neighborhoods, our politics, and our families.

The expectation used to be that young people would marry someone the same as themselves—same race, same socio-economic level, same religion. What this viewpoint failed to recognize was that difference has always been inescapable. Women are different from men. Each individual woman (or man) is different from other women (or men). Educational backgrounds are dissimilar. Personalities and abilities and upbringings have made us different from one another. With changing economics, fortunes can be won or lost overnight or over a lifetime, so social and economic status is unpredictable. Neighborhoods can bring together families with much in common, but always there have been people sharing our larger communities who have been drawn from different backgrounds and, of course, different religions. Today, our greater awareness of the multicultural and multifaith nature of our shrinking planet means that on the streets, in schools, workplaces, and in our own families, we see this diversity. And some find partners who are very different from themselves.

We usually mean by the term "interfaith marriage" the kind of partnership that brings together people of different religions. In times past, these different religions have been suspicious of and possibly even hostile toward each other. Catholics and Protestants, Jews and Christians, Muslims and Hindus, or members of eastern religious faiths and members of western religions, have typically not understood each other well and certainly have not been comfortable living too closely together. In the past, religious communities have not condoned interfaith marriages and interfaith couples have faced opposition and even rejection from fellow believers and family members. Even today, there are religious traditions that actively discourage such partnerships and offer strong grounds for their position. Such convictions lead some communities to forbid their clergy from performing the marriage ceremony or using their places of worship for an interfaith ceremony. Some may even consider the believing partner no longer a member of their faith community.

In her study of the history of families, Beatrice Gottlieb illustrates why this attitude has been important to religions. In her book, *The Family in the Western World,* she suggests that one reason Jews survived centuries of oppression was their religious endogamy, that is, their practice of marrying partners in their faith. Huguenots, though, saw their numbers dwindle after they were outlawed by the state in 1685, because of exogamy; that is, they began to marry out of their tradition. As Paul and Rachel Cowan note in their book, *Mixed Blessings,* Jews today, including those who intermarry, are still concerned about how Judaism will fare as more Jews marry outside of the faith. The memories of the Holocaust are a reminder that the survival of a tradition is tenuous at best.

Drawing on the experiences of families they have worked with, the Cowans illustrate other kinds of fears that make intermarriage seem forbidding (see Key 6). Some are afraid of what will become of their child if he isn't baptized or circumcised in his first few weeks. Others cannot imagine home life without everyone celebrating Christmas or Easter or Ramadan. Some feel pressured by their partners to attend the services of their partner's religion, and then feel like traitors to their own faith if they do attend.

Although it is rare indeed to find a religious group actually encouraging interfaith marriages, many have had to face the reality that their members do find partners from other religious traditions. These religious groups have been prompted to seek ways to minister to these members and support them and their children in their ongoing religious development. In *Mixed Marriages,* Joel Crohn reports that in America, 21% of Catholics, 32% of Jews, 5% of Hindus, 25% of Lutherans, 30% of Mormons, 32% of Episcopalians, 40% of Muslims, and 58% of Buddhists have set up home with a partner of a different faith. These figures are accompanied by a significant decrease in the number of conversions adults undergo to join their partners' religion. Lee Gruzen also notes in *Raising Your Jewish Christian Child* that second marriages are more likely to be interfaith marriages than first ones.

Whether a faith tradition actively discourages interfaith marriages or has adjusted to the reality that large numbers of their members choose partners outside of their faith, they share a common concern that such a home will face an even greater number of tensions at a time when every home and family already has to cope with many stresses of modern life. They know that the tensions and stresses will become even greater with the arrival of a child.

Parents have an important task in finding the best way to nurture their child's spiritual life when they walk different

11

paths of faith. Which religion will they share with their child? How will they enlist the support and help of their family and friends? What kind of compromises will they have to make to accommodate the different wishes of both parents?

Setting up house with partners from different faith traditions is the most obvious kind of interfaith family. In a sense, however, even a couple of the same faith may have an interfaith partnership if one parent is more committed to the beliefs and practices of their faith than the other. How often will the family attend services? What rituals will be performed in the home? Will the child be sent to religious instruction classes or parochial school? How much time, money, and support will the couple and their child give to the religion?

There is yet another kind of interfaith marriage. If one parent is committed to social and humanistic causes that he faithfully works for and believes in and finds all he needs in terms of personal inspiration from nature and working with others, while the other parent finds her spiritual fulfillment and support in the beliefs and practices of a religious community, such a couple must plan for the consequences of different faith journeys.

None of these kinds of family is doomed to failure. But the success of an interfaith marriage is better assured when the couple goes about its tasks of home-building and child-raising with thorough preparation, thoughtful consideration of each other's faith journey, and a willingness on the part of both partners to work together for the good of the child.

4

~~~~~~

FAITH DEVELOPMENT— A TOP PRIORITY

G ood parents provide the things their growing child needs. This is so apparent it hardly needs to be said, despite the occasional news headline to the contrary. When a child comes into the world, so it is said, she brings her love with her and that love impels her parents to take care of her.

Parents provide all that her physical growth requires— nourishing food, exercise, time in the fresh air and sunshine, sufficient sleep, protection from danger, and the knowledge and habits to keep her safe on the streets, in the playground, and at home. She learns how not to speak to strangers, to play safely on the swings, to eat broccoli, to wash her hands before meals, and to go to bed at seven. Her parents undertake this program of teaching and activity so she will grow strong and healthy.

Parents also provide for their child's intellectual growth. They teach her words when she begins to make those first responsive babbling sounds. They give her toys that she will learn to manipulate and even pull apart to put together again. They read her stories and introduce her to books when she begins to read for herself. Where possible, they install learning programs and an encyclopedia on the home computer. They make sure she is enrolled at school and provide a quiet place for her to do her homework. They help her with her projects and keep in touch with her teachers. They talk with her about the world and plan trips to new places. They tune to educational programs on TV. Her parents do all these things so she will grow up to be well-informed, articulate, and wise.

Parents also provide for their child's spiritual growth. Just as they cannot and would not delegate to others their responsibility to provide for the needs of her growing body and mind, so they would not expect others to take over caring for her soul. They endeavor to teach her how to pray, to worship, to learn about God, to be responsive to the needs of others, to care for the environment, to choose good over evil, and to face her fears with confidence and trust. They do this because they want her life to be inspired by faith.

Of course, they do not have to bear the full responsibility of the child's development alone—the community provides parks for exercise, schools for teaching, TV programs for relaxation and education, medical centers and licensed health-care practitioners for treating illness and accident, a police force to maintain public safety, curriculum designers and book publishers for learning programs, as well as synagogues, churches, mosques, and temples for worship. But all these aids and services can only supplement what the child receives at home. The foundation of good health, an alert and receptive mind, and faith, hope, and devotion is most surely given by the parents.

If parents have the same opportunity and duty for their child's spiritual growth as for her physical and mental development, imparting faith to her becomes a top priority, right up there with putting wholesome food on the table and teaching her to look both ways before crossing the street. And developing in faith is as continuous a process as her growing stature and learning new skills. It continues throughout her childhood and into adult life.

All these developments take place best in a consistent and nurturing environment. A child does not become healthy through the occasional breath of fresh air, riding her bicycle safely sometimes, and eating something other than junk food just now and then. A child's mind does not expand intellectually by reading a single book, attending school just one day a week, and only having a stimulating conversation with an adult when granddad comes for his annual visit. Neither does a child grow in faith when her parents are too busy to sit with her and watch in wonder as the sun sets, go with her to services each week, or show her how to say her prayers.

If parents dream for their child that her life will be full of meaning and purpose, that her character will be established on ultimate verities, that her decisions will be guided by a sense of the good, the true, and the beautiful, that she will be motivated by trust, confidence, and hope, then both parents have long-term spiritual work to do with her as she grows. These desirable outcomes cannot be left to chance. Clearly, couples should plan for the spiritual development of their children even before they marry. Interfaith couples have a doubly important responsibility to work out how they will approach the spiritual upbringing of their children.

The faiths of an interfaith couple are rich resources to draw on. Consult them, harmonize them, resolve their differences in some way that is mutually satisfying, make them real ways of believing and trusting in your lives, and let their inspiration be felt in ways that will provide a consistent faith-filled environment for your growing child.

15

5

~~~~~~

GOOD THINGS
ABOUT AN
INTERFAITH FAMILY

An interfaith marriage is not something to be entered into lightly. Since faith helps shape our sense of self, other, and God, couples of sharply different faiths have much to work through. First, they must find the will and the way to live together harmoniously. Every couple has this challenge in terms of family finances, choosing a place to live, arranging work schedules, getting to know the in-laws, choosing vacations, making meals, and even deciding what time to go to bed and who takes charge of the TV. In addition, an interfaith couple has the duty of choosing a religious community, arranging a pattern for attending services, setting up a mutually agreeable program of devotions, agreeing on a plan for giving time and resources to their religious communities, and accepting each other's moral and religious codes of conduct.

Second, interfaith couples must find a mutually agreeable approach to the religious and spiritual education of their children. One or both partners may need to compromise. Some find a way for their religious beliefs and practices to coexist. Some discover that the faith of one partner can accommodate the other partner's faith in some way. Others, finding both of these alternatives impossible, make a clear choice of which faith will be followed. In each case, good things may emerge in this family for the faith development of the child.

• *The child's spiritual development will likely have been carefully thought through.*

Because they have had to deal with their religious differences as their relationship developed, an interfaith couple has usually dealt with religious issues before their first child is born. If one partner is Christian and the other Jewish, for instance, one has probably become newly acquainted with Sabbath services and Jewish family traditions and the other has learned more about Christmas and Easter and become used to weekly attendance at services. Even before they take their vows, they should have worked out a mutually satisfying arrangement for their own religious commitments and settled down to a negotiated routine and a set of shared expectations that meets the needs of both.

In such a home, the child's faith development is less likely to be left to chance. In the process of coming to terms with their own differences, the parents have had a wonderful opportunity to consider what religious affiliation they will encourage and what kinds of observances they will establish in their home. Because they have had to think these issues through, their planning gives their newborn a premeditated environment for growing in faith.

• *The child has the rich resources of two faith traditions on which to build a personal faith.*

Where parents are open to the possibilities of learning from each other despite differences in their faith journeys, the child can be blessed with two traditions of faith. Although they will not want to confuse her with a dizzying array of alternatives, the faith she grows up with will be something like a dialogue between two viewpoints. If the parents of an interfaith home accept that each faith tradition can be a pathway to God, they will encourage her to be open to what both can teach her.

17

Bringing two perspectives into conversation can be seen more as an enrichment than a watering down of faith. Being open to the influences of two faiths is something like being fluent in two languages—each one introduces the child to a different world of possibility and opportunity.

A question arises at this point. Does living with two religious faiths interfere with a child's sense of who she is? Lee Gruzen reported in *Raising Your Jewish/Christian Child* that the children she interviewed from interfaith homes almost invariably described themselves as having a connection with both parents and both religions, regardless of what religion was chosen for or by them. An enthusiastic endorser of the possibilities of interfaith marriages, Gruzen argues that having a way of describing herself is what is important for a child's sense of assurance and identity development, not whether that identity is developed under single or mixed conditions. She found that children brought up in a home with two faiths were sometimes adept at inventing their own identity terms: "Jewlic" or "Ca-Jew" (for Catholic-Jewish), "a patchwork quilt," a "melange," or for one Jewish-Christian child, the rather novel "star-crossed lover" that combines the images of the star of David and the Christian cross. One child with a black Baptist mother and white Jewish father invented the term "Blewish" to describe himself.

Leslie Goodman-Malamuth and Robin Margolis (*Between Two Worlds*), who speak from their own experience as well as their research, remind readers of the other side of the story—that neither the Jewish nor Christian communities has fully worked out quite what to do about these mixed-faith children, and this can be disorienting and disturbing for healthy psychological development. But they too found that these children can be quite creative in finding a label for themselves: "Greek mind; Jewish heart," "a conglomerate," "a recovering Jew," or "semi-Semitic Jewish hillbilly." In other words, a child's religious identity is not necessarily shattered by living in an interfaith home, but can actually take on a concreteness and viability of its own.

Joel Crohn would agree. In a chapter of *Mixed Marriages* entitled, "Split at the Root," he makes the case that if the home has been supportive and not divided in dealing with the growing child's faith journey, the child is more likely to learn that identity and faith is as much a matter of choice and decision as of destiny. In other words, she is less likely to take faith for granted and more likely to assume responsibility for building her own life of faith.

* *The child has a unique opportunity to learn to cope well with people different from himself.*
In a world made up of many different kinds of people, people must learn to live together. Social order, their business dealings, the shared political structures, systems of justice, and the general harmony of communities depends on peoples' ability to accept those others around them. This does not mean they will live without standards and codes of behavior, but they will distinguish between those that are for the common good and those that are personal.

A child who has been raised in a family that is used to recognizing differences, especially the profound differences between dissimilar faiths, respecting them, and learning how to negotiate them, has a distinct advantage in coping with the wider multicultural, multifaith world. At school, in the playground, or in the neighborhood, he is likely to meet different others. An interfaith home is a training ground for learning respect instead of prejudice and accepting personal differences over a desire for mere conformity. It is where he can learn the skills necessary for resolving conflict while maintaining personal integrity. Such a child will grow up to be an asset in a world where people so easily turn hostile against others who believe or act differently.

6

POTENTIAL PROBLEMS FOR AN INTERFAITH FAMILY

There have been very good reasons why many religions have discouraged interfaith marriages. Above and beyond what every other couple must cope with in setting up a new home and family, an interfaith couple has another set of adjustments to make and compromises to forge. Negotiating problems along the way can have two kinds of consequences. Difficulties can be opportunities for creative problem solving, in which case a sense of shared respect and trusting cooperation is deepened. Or they may become occasions for tension and conflict, in which case the partnership is strained and possibly even eroded.

Some of the points of tension that need to be dealt with include:

• *Conflicting views*
An obvious point of contention in an interfaith home is the fundamental disagreements between faiths over a whole range of issues. In *Mixed Matches,* Joel Crohn recalls some of the specific instances that have to be dealt with when different religions and cultural backgrounds share the same living space: a Muslim and a Christian may disagree about gender roles and how sons and daughters should be reared; a

20

Jew and a Protestant may differ on how and what kinds of discipline should be used and the level of emotional expression employed in dealing with each other and their children; a Mexican Catholic and an American Catholic may have a falling out over the central role of the church in their social and family life; a parent may want to pass on the religious and cultural roots of their Asian partner, but the partner prefers to forget these roots and the painful memories these may involve. These are added to the already divergent views each partner may have about the nature of God, what counts as sacred scripture, how worship should be conducted, beliefs about the destiny of believers and non-believers, one's religious duties, and so on.

- *Feeling threatened*

  Basically, because a faith has a wide-sweeping influence on what a person believes, does, and feels, no one makes a long-term commitment to a faith without believing in it. It has the feel of truth and rightness. It is trusted, supported, relied on. It becomes habitual, a way of life, and in fact, it may come to be regarded by individual believers as *the* way of life. So when one faith meets another in an interfaith marriage and has to find common ground, the chances are that both partners are likely to feel at some level threatened over what they consider to be the truth.

  Although there are some religious groups that accept that there are many alternative ways to God, most religions reinforce their sense of rightness by systematizing beliefs as creeds and creating institutions to pass on and preserve their particular faith understandings and practices. Some actively proselytize, seeking to make converts through a variety of outreach programs and conducting religious instruction classes for the young. An anticipated outcome of believing one's religion is true is coming to believe that other traditions are false. Through the centuries, there have been

Jews who have not accepted that God has any special relationship with Gentiles, Christians who take literally the words of the Bible that no one can come to God except through Jesus, and Muslims who regard others as having an incomplete and imperfect understanding of the will of God. A home with one or both partners who believe strongly that their faith is the only right one will obviously face more conflicts than those whose beliefs are more inclusive.

While feeling confused or left out or even threatened may happen any time, there are occasions when it can be particularly acute. Although Morris comes from a Muslim family, he agreed with Barbara to raise any children they might have as Christian, but when their first daughter was christened he felt like a mere bystander at the service, especially when all the Christian relatives and friends were full participants in the ceremonies and came back to the home afterwards for a celebration. He also didn't foresee how it might feel for him when Barbara insisted that their children be sent to a Christian school. At some deep level he had a sense of being rejected by those closest to him because of his Muslim faith.

• *Being pulled in two directions at once*
In interfaith homes, many parents may want to follow their own faith but also support their partner's faith. They may hope that their child will accept their faith, but do not want to isolate her from the values and beliefs of their partner. They may want to be accepting of their partner's beliefs and practices, but also harbor a secret hope to win them over to their own faith some day. Margie admits that she married Don knowing full well that he was not interested in religion or going to church. Nevertheless, he was so understanding and reasonable, she fully expected she would have plenty of opportunity to talk to him and gradually get him to go along to church with her. Don, however, never wanted to talk reli-

gion, and didn't ever show any interest in going to church with her. Margie often went to church with her eyes stinging with tears, in part because they had disagreed again over the issue and in part because she feared he would be lost from God. So it is not unusual for partners dealing with two ways of living to feel divided loyalties and commitments.

If parents can feel torn, it is easy to imagine how much more children will feel the opposing forces. As children of interfaith families, Leslie Goodman-Malamuth and Robin Margolis describe themselves as being born into "two worlds" (*Between Two Worlds*). They admit that throughout their lives and despite their choice for one religion over another, they could never totally sever all ties with both. Always they felt a degree of conflict over their decisions, internally and externally, and struggled to balance the pull of these divided loyalties. They also describe the overwhelming sadness children can feel, even as preschoolers, at being not quite like other children whose parents share the same faith.

While a child's parents may be open to their partner's religious faith, not all the members of the extended family may be as accepting. In a study of the grown children of interfaith homes, the Cowans reported that some people realized they were being protected from and/or exposed to grandparents who were fervent in their particular faith. Some of these adults recalled occasions when they felt a rush of jealousy or hurt when cousins from the same faith as the grandparents' were favored over them. Some remembered having to listen to ethnic and religious slights about their faith or that of other members of their extended families.

- *Using religion as a tool for manipulating others*
In any relationship, forces are at work, some drawing people closer together, others pulling them apart. When a relationship of two becomes a family of three, the forces become

even more complex. There are times when the three function as a unit: all agree, all work together, all accept how things are or what direction they want to move in. But there are other times when one is at odds with the other two, or even when each one is at odds with the others. These dynamics, fluctuating day by day, week by week, and year by year, are quite normal and natural. The rosy days of falling in love and rejoicing over the arrival of a baby are followed by the months and years of negotiating the realities of living in interacting force fields.

Into this dynamic, religion comes with its passions, its commitments, and its practices. Even when the family lives by the same faith, and seems to draw on the same hopes, philosophy, beliefs, and responses, there can be significant differences to deal with as each member makes his or her own interpretations and comes to value different aspects of their mutual faith. But when two or more faiths exist side by side, the partners' fundamentally different hopes, beliefs, and practices can become even more divided. In this situation, a child may learn how to play one parent against another, or one parent plays the child against the other parent, and so on. Religion can then become a tool for manipulating family members to get one's own way.

For example, Bryan had been brought up Jewish, but like Julie, his Christian wife, he had not been a practicing member of his community. Over the years, he had been preoccupied with his work, and had left the child-rearing largely to Julie. As his first son, Matt, approached adolescence, he began to sense he was a stranger to his children. He decided to win Matt's favor by sponsoring the boy's bar mitzvah, even over the complaints of his wife. Julie always maintained that he used religion to try to win his son's affection while driving a wedge between her and the boy. Negotiating the dynamic of family living without appearing to resort to religious pieties can be a real challenge.

Many early studies of interfaith homes suggested that the net effect of all the opposing religious forces on children is that they grow to maturity maladjusted, with identity problems, feelings of alienation, anxiety, and low self-esteem. However, several more recent writers, some of whom speak from personal experience, do not agree that these outcomes are inevitable. Given the growing acceptance of interfaith marriages and taking into account the success stories as well as the problem cases, there are parenting practices that not only cope with the differences but capitalize on them.

7

~~~~~~

PREPARING YOURSELF

When planning to be married, there is no better place to begin your preparations than with yourself. As Shakespeare wisely wrote, "This above all: to thine own self be true." The problem is, though, that while most everyone would agree that they want to be true to themselves, they don't know who they are. How can you be true to yourself, when "yourself" is a stranger?

Excited about the prospect of getting married, stressed about finding the right place to live, getting to know the in-laws, planning the wedding details, resolving any career-track collisions, wanting but not always getting the approval of all your family and friends—taken together, all this can fill every waking moment of an engaged couple. And even when you look back to how your life was before you met each other, it was filled to overflowing with other concerns, interests, occupations, and responsibilities. The pace and pressures of life leave very little time for getting to know yourself.

But, getting to know yourself is significant for anybody, particularly important for those about to link their lives with somebody else, and absolutely essential if that somebody else is from a different faith. Shakespeare tells us why this process is vital when he goes on to say, "And it must follow, as the night the day,/Thou canst not then be false to any man." If we take these words and apply them to the couple contemplating marriage, he might well be saying: "If you want an open, trusting, honest, enduring, authentic relationship, then as inevitably as day follows night, it depends on being open, trusting, honest, enduring, and authentic with yourself!"

Getting to know yourself and being true to yourself is intimately connected with faith. It means discovering what you believe and feel, deep down inside, about the meaning of life, moral duty, hope, trust, commitment, relationships—and living in such a way that you do not betray these beliefs and feelings. Together these qualities define who you really are. They are your faith.

Much of the time, especially when you are with people who believe and feel much the same way as you do, you take these things for granted because they are so much a part of you. They rise up and demand your attention usually only when you face some crisis or change in your life. But when this entity "you," with beliefs and feelings about the big issues of life, is about to set up a lifelong partnership with another entity, "your beloved," with all his or her beliefs and feelings about these issues, and knowing that these are drawn from a different well of faith than your own, then you both need to give them close personal scrutiny.

Coming to know yourself is a major undertaking, sometimes a struggle, that unfolds over a lifetime, but well worth the effort. Without the effort, a person will live what might be called a "two-dimensional" life—flat and superficial. With the effort, a person can live "three-dimensionally"—more deeply, more meaningfully, more thoughtfully. There are some things to do that will help you in this process, some of which apply only to yourself, some of which will help you reach out beyond yourself.

▲▲

- *Ask the big questions.*

  These are the questions that cannot be answered in a moment but grow in power and meaning over the years. Set aside some quiet spaces in your life to reflect on them.
  — What are the things I trust most?
  — What do I have to hold on to when everything in my world seems to be going wrong?
  — What makes me most content?
  — What community of people in my life make me feel secure, at home?
  — What is the direction I want my life to take?
  — Why am I here?
  — Who am I?
  — What are my dreams for my child? My nightmares?

- *Ask the practical questions.*

  These are the questions that relate specifically to the kinds of issues that can come up between people of different faiths.
  — What elements of my faith tradition do I cherish and would never want to give up?
  — How important is it to me to maintain my connection with my faith tradition?
  — What is my attitude to and belief about other people's religions?
  — What religious or faith practices would I always want to be able to do at home and with my community?
  — How would I cope with always having to do these things without my partner?
  — What would I dearly want my child to be able to participate in?
  — What would I be comfortable allowing my child to do with my partner?
  — How will I feel if my partner never changes her attitude about my faith?

— How will I feel if my partner never changes his attitude about his faith?

— If you are the child of an interfaith home, what legacy do you value and what pitfalls would you want to avoid when it comes to dealing with your own child?

• *Keep a journal.*
A journal is more than a calendar of events—it is the story of your personal journey. Here you can ask yourself the big questions about the meaning of life and address the practical questions of making a home with a partner of a different faith. Writing down your thoughts as you go can help you focus and give you something to do as you reflect, while prompting you to make your ideas clear. Most of all, it is a place where you can examine your inner life honestly, without the pressure of pleasing somebody else. As you read back over your own history, this record of your progress will reveal patterns in your own thinking that you would not have guessed were there and show you which loose ends still need to be tied off, especially if you are the product of an interfaith home.

• *Find advisors to talk with.*
While personal discovery is something you can only do for yourself, trusted others can help you in the process. A minister, rabbi, teacher, or priest who knows you or understands your background is trained and experienced in this role. A close friend, a parent, or somebody else who cares for you can be a good sounding board to try out your questions and ideas. Since most people you might speak with will have their own biases and fears about your impending choice of partner, many couples actively seek out other interfaith couples who can speak from their own experiences. Some find a good conversation partner or community of people undertaking a similar venture through web pages and the Internet. Some of these are given in the Suggested Readings and Resources at the end of this book.

- *Seek out a good resource.*

  No matter where you live you can have access to some of the most profoundly spiritual people the world has known— through their writings. Other people have taken this journey of self-discovery and have been willing to share their experience. You will find their writings in libraries and bookstores everywhere. Some particularly valuable references are listed under Suggested Readings and Resources at the end of this book.

- *Make time.*

  Being true to yourself, discovering yourself, cannot be undertaken in haste. It requires quiet reflection over time. If you are a morning person, you might plan to get up early, take a cup of coffee into a sunny spot in the house, and work on your journal before the demands of the day begin pressing in on you. If you are a night person, you might choose to have a solitary evening at home with the TV off so you can do some serious reading. Getting to this important work for most people means they have to plan it and make a time for it.

8

^^

PREPARING
TOGETHER

O ne of the most significant, life-shaping steps an interfaith couple can take is to confront their differences in
faith and find a way to deal with them—before they have
even decided where to live and certainly before having a child.
Leaving this negotiation till after the birth of a child, or even
after you have set up home, may very well make for a rude
awakening.

Janet, whose upbringing and faith commitment revolved
around a fundamentalist Christian church, and Mark, who was
loosely affiliated to a mainline Protestant congregation, were
making wedding plans and looking forward to a happy life together. Janet's father, who was a lay leader in his church, happened to ask them one day what they had decided to do about
their future children's religious involvement. An insightful
question from a concerned father!

Janet immediately responded by saying they were going
to sort out any religious issues when the need arose—maybe
when a baby was on the way. Until then, things would continue
the way they were: She would go to her church as always and
Mark would come along with her as often as he wanted, although he would go to his own church for special occasions.
She imagined that religion might be more of an issue for her
than him, so any child they might have would probably be
brought up in her church and enroll in the church school.

Mark's jaw dropped with surprise. He hadn't been thinking this way. In fact, he wasn't thinking much about religious matters at all. Somewhere in the back of his mind, though, he imagined that after they were married, Janet would not only leave her parents' home, but also their church. The two of them would instead find a new church that they both would feel comfortable in. He even suspected that they would be so engaged in setting up a new home together, while at the same time maintaining their careers and other interests, that religion would hardly be an issue.

Now religion was out on the table. They discovered that even choosing a minister to perform the marriage was a question that had to be addressed. Janet and Mark had very long, serious, and sometimes stressful, discussions after that. In the end, Mark agreed that he would be comfortable with the kind of Christian upbringing Janet had in mind for their child, although he would not join the church himself. They would not plan to send the child to church school, but they agreed to look at the matter of schooling again when they knew where they would be living at the time their child came of school age. They were married later that year, by two ministers, incidentally, one from each congregation. One can only imagine how much misunderstanding and disagreement Janet and Mark may have brought on themselves had they not sorted out some of these things beforehand. Given the demands of meeting house payments, resolving conflicting work schedules and career opportunities, and making the myriad other adjustments couples face when they set up house together, at least this area of potential conflict had been openly discussed and prepared for.

The particular choice Janet and Mark made is not right for every couple, but the important point is that they sorted out their preferences and differences before they were married. Some couples, unable to reach a consensus on these issues, have the luxury of deciding against marriage to avoid living with intolerable or stressful conditions for them and their children. Janet and Mark and countless other couples, however, do negotiate their differences and find common ground. But it takes some forethought and planning. In his book *Mixed Matches,* Joel Crohn observes that the "perfect couple," who suddenly and mysteriously split up after many years, may very often be the one that got too good at avoiding the tough issues, until the relationship could no longer be sustained. In other words, a couple needs to confront their differences and plan together. Here are some suggestions.

• *Get to know your partner's faith.*
Most people gather some impressions and facts about other religions, but these are not always accurate or complete. Paul and Rachel Cowan, who conducted numerous workshops for Jewish-Christian interfaith couples, listed some of the things these partners are not likely to know about each other's faith. They found that most of the Jewish partners had never read any of the New Testament; Christian partners had usually read the Old Testament but in the context of their own religion and without the benefit of Jewish commentaries. Most Jews know what Christmas and Easter celebrate, but not Advent or Lent and how they are observed. Christians have usually learned about Passover in Sunday School, but do not know why matzoh is served and bread is avoided. They know about the candles and gift-giving of Hanukkah but not what the holiday commemorates. The picture is further complicated, these researchers note, when even the partner who ascribes to a particular faith does not know it well.

To make a good plan with a partner, each one needs to be well informed, not only about what he or she believes and does, but also about what the other believes and does. By keeping an open mind, you can find opportunities to experience your partner's religion firsthand. Where possible, you might attend services, join the young peoples' group, participate with your partner's family in their annual celebrations, delve into reading matter that you might find on the subject, and ask your partner and the wider family and friends lots of questions. Another's religion may seem strange and even threatening at first, but on better acquaintance, you may come to realize that the journey of faith has many forms. In fact, you may find you will gain new insights from another's faith that will enrich your own perspective and help you better appreciate your partner's religion.

- *Seek advice from trusted counselors.*

Apart from what you can learn firsthand, there are others who are well experienced in matters of faith, and from what they have undergone or learned, they may have helpful advice to share with you. Your parents may be a good starting point. Consider also talking things over with a valued religious counselor. Many religious communities hold classes for couples intending to marry and set up support groups especially for interfaith couples. Trusted friends from your congregation, especially those who have enjoyed a successful relationship with a spouse of a different faith, may be good advice-givers as well. It is helpful if you and your partner can meet with these counselors together. Ask your questions and raise your doubts, hopes, and fears, so that together you may weigh your choices and seek your solutions.

- *Be honest with your partner.*

As you work your way toward consensus, above all else be honest. Share with your partner what your non-negotiables are. What events would you want to participate in—weekly services, yearly convocations, fasting periods, or outreach activities? Does your faith permit you to participate in another's religious celebrations? What rituals would you really want your child to experience? What financial commitments (offerings, tithes, and other gifts) would you want to continue to make to your religious organization? Who or what will you continue to accept as influential in your life—your religious leaders, sacred writings, your religious family? Not only should you be open in telling your partner what your needs and hopes are, but you should be just as open in listening to your partner's needs and hopes as well.

- *Grant each other religious freedom.*
With an array of information now at your disposal, together you can begin to see if your two religious lives can mesh together. Consensus is not usually reached immediately but is something you work toward step by step through ongoing conversations and sharings. From the honest discussions you will have had, it will be apparent to you what elements in your religious lives are fixed and what are more flexible. Together, develop a workable schedule that accommodates both religious lives. Do not coerce or manipulate each other, but allow your partner's religious life to flourish as he or she would wish. Unless you can treat with respect your partner's faith journey, your child will inevitably be caught in some kind of cross fire between you.

- *Make a plan for your child.*
The choices you make for your child are different from the choices you will make about your own religious life. You have your faith. You have a tradition and an upbringing and a lifetime of decisions and choices that have shaped your religious journey. Unless one of you has converted from your faith to that of your partner's (as is sometimes done), or you have both converted from your separate faiths to a commonly chosen new faith (which is rarely done), you will be an interfaith family.

The plan you make for your child may be in line with

one or the other parent's faith, or a mix of both, or altogether different from both. Over weeks or months or even years, talk things over, look at the pros and cons of particular choices as they apply to your situation, get advice, share openly and honestly, until you find common ground.

In this process, you might "try on" the various choices by imagining them as different scenarios in which you picture all the characters involved and think through all the implications. A non-Jewish partner might imagine Rosh Hashanah, members of the family in the synagogue, the fasting, and the seriousness of this time of self-reflection; a non-Christian might think about Christmas with its carols, church services, and gift-giving; a non-Muslim might picture the day divided by times for prayer and the change in the daily routine of meals during Ramadan—and in these instances, how they see themselves reacting and responding.

Your final plan for your child's upbringing will take shape and feel right for you both—if you give it time to evolve. It will mean finding the kind of compromises that are most comfortable for you both, possibly giving up some cherished hopes or desires, and probably assuming some responsibilities or attitudes previously unanticipated.

If this point seems unreachable, then you would be wise to give up your plans to set up house together. These problematic differences are among the most serious a couple will face, so when they are left unresolved, a lifetime of conflict awaits. Throughout, be guided by what you consider to be of optimal benefit first for your child, then for you, and finally for your wider circle of friends, family, and religious community.

• *Resolve to remain open to the process of working things out between you.*

At best, the future can be discerned only dimly. Life brings surprises even to the best-planned relationships. Changes in location, crises in faith, altered family dynamics when children join the home, and other unanticipated developments along the way can reshape and mature your early perspectives. If you look on the plans you make together for bringing up your child as your best effort at the time, you leave open the option of allowing these plans to adapt to your family's inevitable transitions. Develop early the habit of being able to talk things through empathetically, honestly, and judiciously so that your plans might grow and adapt in harmony with your changing experiences.

9

〰〰

PREPARING FAMILY AND FRIENDS

No family exists in a vacuum—even though the large extended family with several generations and close relatives living together has been largely replaced by the nuclear family made up of mother, father, and their children. And even the nuclear family is not as widespread as one might think with so many single-parent families, alternative family structures, and many individuals living alone for one reason or another. Yet even in the most fractured circumstances, every parent and every child is connected with others and influenced by them. Because human beings are social creatures, we identify those to whom we are related and develop connections with friends and acquaintances.

This network of family and friends provides a context in which parenting and growing up take place. It is not only inescapable, but also indispensable. Human beings need each other to learn, to communicate, to discover values and undertake moral actions, to find companionship, and to develop a sense of self. In other words, we need family and friends, and they need us. In this mutual interconnectedness, what we do affects others and what they do affects us.

When an interfaith couple declare their intent to set up a home and raise a family, they bring two worlds of family and friends together, along with all the hopes, wishes, and expectations of both. Because these two worlds will probably be very different, it is often a challenge for the couple to find acceptance and backing for their choice of partner from all sides. And yet, they cannot comfortably shrug off the dissenting or disagreeable voices in these worlds without suffering some personal loss as well. Ideally, they would prefer to have the support of all those near and dear to them because the decisions they will make in bringing up their child will meet with some kind of response from those around them. Better if that response is informed and sympathetic, than alienated and hostile.

While a couple cannot be responsible for the actions and reactions of those close to them, they can at least attempt to gain the support and respect of their family and friends. Preparing the circle of people around them for their interfaith home is a task that needs to be considered along with engagement announcements, wedding plans, and choosing a place to live. These guidelines might encourage you to do this kind of preparation thoroughly.

- *Identify those who will be closest to you in your new role as spouse and parent.*
When Ahmed was planning to marry Jeanette, he knew his family in Iran had a particular interest in his fiancée, for he was Muslim and she was Christian. His family expected him to bring any children he might have back to his home country where the child would be raised in the faith of Islam, and Jeanette concurred. Jeanette's friends had mixed reactions when they first heard the news, although her very closest friends were quick to be supportive and willing to give suggestions. They then each began to share their news with a wider circle of friends, acquaintances, and family members. By the day of the wedding, everybody who they felt should know had been informed and so they began life together with nothing hidden from people who might one day be needed for their understanding of and respect for their choice of life partner.

- *Listen to your friends and family.*
  Sometimes this will be difficult. Some family members may be very outspoken against the idea of your setting up house with somebody of a different faith. They may fret and nag about how the children will be brought up. They may distance themselves from you. Joel Crohn makes the point that not all the opposition an interfaith couple may encounter can be simply reduced to bigotry. The response may come from a genuine concern that the respective partners be able to maintain the integrity of their faith. It may reflect the distress of the families over the disruption or breakdown of the extended family. In other cases, the family may be guarded but attempt to reach out in friendship and support to your partner and your plans, and their awkwardness at doing so will be evidence of the strain they are feeling (*Mixed Matches*). In still other cases, your close circle of friends and family may be wholeheartedly understanding and encouraging from the beginning. Whatever the reaction, remember that, in their own way, all these people care for you and want your ultimate happiness. Their responses are an expression of this care. Listen for insights that can be invaluable to you in your planning.
- *Allow time for your family and friends to adjust to your news and plans.*
  Parents and others cherish dreams for you and how your life will unfold. When you deviate from that (and inevitably most of us do), they must cope with a measure of surprise and even disappointment. These emotions are likely to be more intense over your choice of partner than almost anything else you will do in your life. Give them time to come to terms with your news. On acquaintance, especially if you are happy and seem well suited as a couple, some of the immediate shock will be ameliorated. Couples have been known to overhear comments like, "Josh is a lovely boy—even though he

is Jewish!" or, "Mary might be a Gentile, but she does bake good challah!" Of course, in some cases, the reverse may happen. However, probably by the wedding day, and even more likely, by the birth of your first child, your steadfastness may have at least made your ongoing relationship with reluctant family members at least predictable. More often than not, even those that have opposed your choices, can be trusted for help if you should ever need it.

• *Invite the support of family and friends.*
As you share your plans for your child's religious upbringing with your circle of family and friends, indicate to them ways they can be involved in the process and encourage their participation. For instance, they might attend a christening or Brit milah, celebrate a special season with you in your home or theirs, or supervise the child's prayers or other rituals when they baby-sit for you. As they come to know your child's religious community, and of course, come to know and love your child, any lingering hostilities or doubts they might have may melt away. Children have a way of bringing their love with them. If old friends and family members feel shut out of your lives or the life of your child, you may have given them a reason, however unjustifiable, to be unsupportive or critical of your efforts at building an interfaith household.

These guidelines may seem to be lopsided because they encourage you to make all the moves. However, since your choices and plans are the foundation of your interfaith home, it is appropriate to see the initiative resting with you. You will need to do the informing; you will need the wisdom and the courage to stand by your plans for your family's sake; and you may need to put extra effort into winning the support of those around you. Their response to your reaching out is their responsibility and decision, but the originating efforts are clearly yours.

Part Two

∿∿

KNOWING WHAT
TO EXPECT

I f you are contemplating setting up house with a partner of
a different faith tradition than your own, or planning for
the religious development of your child in a faith that is not
familiar to you, you need to know what to expect. In the following keys, you will find a sketch of some of the significant features of various faith traditions—what they believe, how they
worship, what practices are performed in the home, how children are taught the faith, and what rites of passage are celebrated.

Of necessity, these sketches can only serve as a general
introduction. Religions undergo changes and form new congregations that differ from each other across times and cultures. In all the major world religions today, there are a number
of branches, some more traditional, others more contemporary; some more conservative, others more liberal; some more
concerned with particular beliefs, others with particular practices, still others with particular political, social, or cultural
ties. Only some of the major streams within a faith are described here—in fact, Christianity, which has the greatest
number of branches in the western world, is outlined in three
chapters—but no religion in all its complexity can be covered
fully. However, you will glean enough information to know better what to expect and what further details you should seek to
complete your knowledge.

10

GROWING UP JEWISH

Judaism is the oldest monotheistic world religion, tracing its roots back to Abraham of Biblical times and basing its beliefs and practice on the writings known as the Torah. As in most religions, there is not a single form of Judaism, and today one finds Orthodox (including Hasidic), Conservative, Reform, and Reconstructionist Jewish congregations. Like most religions, and perhaps even more than most, Judaism is not merely a religion—it has a cultural, social, and political history and identity as well.

What Jews Believe

Given the wide variety of Jewish communities, no single body of doctrine is accepted by all Jews, although three central ideas largely shape Jewish thought.

The first of these is the idea of *God.* God is always spoken of as one God, rather than many. Many practicing Jews will recite at least twice a day the declaration of faith in God's existence and unity found in Deuteronomy 6:4, "Hear, O Israel, the Lord our God, the Lord is one." Appreciating that God is unique, a Jew is careful about speaking names for God and avoids the four-letter proper name, YHWH, since the correct pronunciation is believed to have been lost. No images of God are permitted and any references to God's physical being are taken as metaphors because Jews believe God is without any physical properties.

The second defining element of Judaism is the *Torah.* This is God's revelation to Moses for humankind. The Torah itself is the five books of Moses, but when the term is used in the broader sense of teaching, Torah includes all of Jewish law, both oral and written. These laws and teachings describe a distinctive worldview and way of life. Written on scrolls, copies of the Torah are housed in Jewish places of worship referred to as temples, synagogues, or *schuls.* The Torah is read during services and Jewish religious education is devoted to its careful study. A rich scholarly tradition has grown up around the Torah and become part of it.

A third central idea in Judaism is the notion of *Israel.* As this idea is used today, it applies at a number of levels. It indicates the original family of Abraham and Sarah, with their descendants. To these people God gave the Torah and the land of Israel. It also refers to the inheritors of the holy way of life described in the Torah, and the community of Jews wherever they live. Today the name also refers to the State of Israel. In Jewish thought, everyone is born a child of God and has a role to play; similarly, those born Jewish have a unique role as people of Israel.

Attitude to Interfaith Marriages

No single attitude characterizes all Jewish views of interfaith marriage, but the preference is for Jews to marry Jews to perpetuate Judaism. However, it is estimated that about half of all Jews in North America marry someone outside of Judaism. When this occurs, a traditional Jewish wedding is usually not performed because, unless both partners are bound by the Torah, the vows made with reference to the laws of Moses are not appropriate. Some rabbis will perform an interfaith marriage service under certain conditions, such as when the couple intends to raise their children Jewish or the non-believing partner plans to convert. A small number of rabbis will participate in a joint wedding service with a clergy member of another faith. A non-Jewish partner cannot be buried with a Jewish spouse in a traditional Jewish funeral service. According to tradition, a child is considered Jewish if the child's mother is Jewish, although in the Reform and Reconstructionist movements, patriarchal descent is also considered if the child is raised as a Jew and makes public affirmation about his or her Jewish identity.

In Jewish belief, marriage is a sacred institution and bringing children into the world is the highest calling. For this reason, Jewish families devote a great deal of time and effort to their children's upbringing, education, and well-being— tasks that optimally depend on the commitment of both parents. Furthermore, many synagogue services have home and community components as well.

Jewish Life

In the home, the child is the central focus and here the stage is set for growing up Jewish. While the particular practices that a family performs vary according to the tradition the parents follow, the present trend is toward rediscovering and reclaiming rituals in family life. Often requiring a time for preparation of heart and home, the ceremonies usually involve lighting candles, singing, offering blessings, reaching out to friends or strangers, and eating traditional or symbolic foods. Among the most common celebrations and holidays are:

> *Shabbat* (the Sabbath)—the one day of the week devoted to rest and reflection, celebrated from sunset Friday to sunset Saturday. There are special rituals for welcoming and closing Shabbat.
> *Rosh Hashanah* (New Year) and *Yom Kippur* (Day of Atonement)—an annual ten-day period for reflection

and soul searching. These are the most solemn Jewish holy days, bringing more Jews to the synagogues than any other day of the year.

Sukkot (Festival of Booths)—a week-long festival celebrating harvest, during which families may choose to live and/or eat in a temporary hut (open to the sky) recalling those used by earlier harvesters.

Hanukkah—a relatively minor holiday that celebrates a military victory and a miracle. Coming in December, Hanukkah has different rituals and meanings from Christmas and should be considered distinct from the Christian celebration.

Purim—a rowdy celebration with costumes, masks, noise-makers, and gift-giving that commemorates the deliverance of the Jews from Haman as recorded in the book of Esther.

Passover—an eight-day spring holiday that recalls the deliverance of the Jews from slavery in Egypt. No leaven is found in the household over this period to recall the hasty leaving when families had no time to prepare leavened bread. The Passover meal or *Seder* is one of the most significant in the year and includes a ritual plate of a number of symbolic foods including bitter herbs, reminding the participants of the bitterness of slavery.

Significant moments in the passage of life are also marked by celebratory rituals. These ceremonies bond the young person and the community. Among the most significant are:

Brit Milah—the circumcision of an eight-day-old baby boy or a new convert to Orthodox or Conservative forms of Judaism. At this time the child is given a Hebrew name and blessings are said. Circumcision signifies the covenant between God and the Jewish people. Performed by a trained *mohel,* the service is a time for celebration with family and friends, and includes liturgical prayers and readings from the Torah, all followed by a festive meal.

Brit Hat-Hayim—a ceremony to indicate a covenant of life for an eight-day-old baby girl. She receives her Hebrew name and is welcomed into Jewish life. This ceremony is usually performed in the synagogue.

Bar Mitzvah (for boys)/*Bat Mitzvah* (for girls in some congregations)—a ceremony that inducts 13-year-old boys and 12- to 13-year-old girls into full-fledged membership in the Jewish community. At this time, the young person is expected to meet all the requirements and observe the practices of the congregation. As an indication of acceptance into the community, the young person is usually invited to read the weekly Torah portion and comment on it. Family and friends celebrate the occasion and sometimes give the boy or girl a prayer shawl or *talit.* A special meal follows the service.

Many Jews also follow a set of dietary laws that describe what can be eaten, how foods, especially meats, are to be prepared, and what combinations of food are proper. *Kosher* foods are those that are permissible—a diet that is a healthy one and also instills a respect for living creatures and the relationship of humans to them.

In a Jewish home one might notice *mezzuzim,* small holders or boxes on the door-posts containing parchment paper upon which is written in Hebrew a declaration of God's existence and oneness. A *Seder* plate for symbolic Passover foods and a *menorah,* or branched candlestick, used at Hanukkah are other evidences of Jewish practice. No images of

God will decorate the home and, since human beings are believed to be in the image of God, tattoos and, for some, body piercings (for rings) are actively discouraged.

The Jewish way of life is well summed up in the prayer offered at the birth of a baby. The traditional prayer is that the child will grow into a life characterized by Torah (learning), the *chupah* (the wedding canopy, which is a symbol of love, commitment, and family), and *ma'asim tovim* (good deeds—giving to the poor, acts of loving kindness, and efforts toward peace and freedom).

11

^^^

GROWING UP CATHOLIC

C hristian communities spread rapidly from Jerusalem after the death of Jesus. Over time, as the church settled matters of doctrine, morality, and church organization, the leaders in Rome garnered the reputation of being solid in the faith and gradually assumed control of the whole church. In the eleventh century, a schism occurred between the churches in the East and West, creating two branches in Christianity—the eastern Orthodox church and western Catholicism. Another split occurred as a result of the Protestant movement of the sixteenth century. Roman Catholicism, so named for remaining loyal to the pope in Rome, is today the largest segment of Christianity. In the recent mid-sixties, church authorities met in a series of sessions known as the Second Vatican Council to re-express the old traditions in ways more relevant to the modern world. At that time, many changes were introduced in attitude and practice, seen especially in the liturgy, the church's relationship to other faiths, the role of the lay person, and a new emphasis on issues of social justice.

What Catholics Believe

Like the Judaism in which Christianity finds its roots, Christians in general accept the notion of a single God. However, they also hold that God is revealed to humanity as a Trinity of beings—the Father, the Son, and the Holy Spirit. Jesus

Christ, the Son, is believed to be the incarnation of God, who came into the world as a man so that through his perfect life and death he could reveal God and save human beings from eternal death because of their sinfulness. The Holy Spirit is God's intimate presence, empowering people to live sanctified lives and to serve God and others.

The church is regarded as the family of God, and the Pope, by tracing his authority back to Peter, a disciple of Jesus, is God's representative who preserves and guides the church. In his role as head of the church, he is influential around the world, and considered infallible when he speaks *ex cathedra* on issues of faith and morals. Mary, who was the mother of Jesus, is considered to be the mother of God. Born a human, she nevertheless is believed to have been immaculate from conception and to have lived perfectly. She was taken up to heaven at the end of her life, where she receives the devotion of believers and is thought to nurture them in the faith. The authority of the Pope, the meaning of some of the sacraments, and this understanding of the role of Mary are key issues separating Catholics from other Christian groups.

Attitude to Interfaith Marriages

In the Catholic view, marriage is sacred. Believing the oneness of the couple is part of the same mystery as the oneness between Christ and the church, Catholics include a celebration of the Mass as part of the wedding ceremony. However, like other religious groups, they are seeing more of their members marry someone of a different faith. Since non-Catholics are not permitted to participate in the Eucharist, the normal wedding service poses problems both for the church and the people attending. It is usually recommended that a scriptural marriage ceremony be performed in place of the Nuptial Mass.

While admitting that interfaith marriages are becoming more common, the Catholic church nevertheless conducts such a wedding service under certain conditions. An official document, "Declaration and Promise by the Catholic Party," may be presented to the Catholic partner beforehand. It basically requires the church member to indicate his or her intention to abide by two basic statements: that he or she intends to continue living as a faithful member of the Catholic Church; and, that he or she promises to do all in his or her power to have any children baptized and raised as Catholics. It is clear from this general policy that while interfaith marriages are a fact of modern life, the Catholic church does not want to lose either Catholic members or their children from the faith.

Catholic Life

Nurturing children in the faith is considered one of the most serious responsibilities parents have and home life is highly regarded. Valuing human life in the official Catholic view means that abortion and most family planning practices are not condoned, although these are contentious issues among members today. The church operates a large parochial school system that attracts Catholic and non-Catholic students. Originally the schools were staffed with members of various religious orders, but today more lay people and even some non-Catholic teachers are employed. Most schools do not require students to attend religious services although some religious instruction is usually mandatory. Emphasizing character development and a rigorous curriculum, Catholic schools attract many children of different faiths. Where there is no parochial school, the church usually operates a strong religious education program for children.

In some cultural groups, including many Hispanic, the church is a focal point in the social and religious life of the people. A Catholic home may display a crucifix and religious paintings or a picture of the Pope. Members are encouraged to study and learn the teachings of the Bible—the Catholic scriptures are somewhat larger than other Christian versions because they contain some additional books known as the Apocrypha. A rosary, or string of beads used as a counting device in repetitive prayers, is sometimes used.

When praying or entering the church, Catholics will make the sign of the cross. In the church vestibule is a bowl of holy water from which they will mark their foreheads with a cross, recalling their baptism. Around the church are fourteen plaques or pictures known as the "stations of the cross" which depict incidents from Jesus' last days. Believers move from one to the other in succession praying and meditating, especially during the Holy Week that commemorates the same events.

In their religious lives, Catholics celebrate a number of sacraments or rituals. These include:

Mass or the Eucharist—celebration of the Last Supper of Christ with bread and wine that serve as the body and blood of Christ. To participate, a member must not eat or drink anything for at least an hour beforehand. Services are held daily in many parishes, although Sunday services are the primary ritual in Catholic life.

Baptism—a ceremony in which water is poured on the forehead, marking the initiation of the recipient into the church, the family of God. Performed for babies and new adult members, it is thought to bind the person to God forever in an unbreakable bond.

Confirmation—a ceremony that initiates the believer into full membership in the church. The bishop anoints the forehead of the young person or adult with oil, tracing the sign of the cross.

Reconciliation—steps taken to celebrate God's forgiveness for sins. Reconciliation services are held for individuals or congregations to mark their intention to turn away from wrongdoing and free themselves from guilt and resentment by the power of the Holy Spirit.

Holy Days—Catholics observe Sundays which commemorate the resurrection of Jesus, and a number of other holy days including, Mary, Mother of God, January 1; Ascension Thursday, forty days after Easter, which commemorates Christ's return to heaven; Mary's Assumption, August 15, commemorating Mary's entry into heaven; All Saints' Day, November 1; Mary's Immaculate Conception, December 8; and Christmas, December 25. Other days are set aside in the official church calendar as fast days in which only one full meal and two lighter meals are permitted and/or abstinence days in which no meat is to be eaten. These include Ash Wednesday and Good Friday (occasions commemorating events around the death of Christ), and in some circles, all other Fridays.

The men and women who dedicate their lives to the church and enter a religious order are celibate, so that they may perform their duties unencumbered. They serve as parish priests, missionaries, and teachers; many work on behalf of the poor and oppressed. Increasingly, lay people are contributing to the church's mission, serving as volunteers, professional workers, and church leaders. While the church continues to wrestle with matters to do with the authority of the Pope, family planning, divorce, celibacy, and the role of women, it continues to flourish world-wide.

12

GROWING UP
PROTESTANT

B eginning with Martin Luther in the sixteenth century, a reformation was launched within the Catholic church over perceived church abuses, political struggles, and theological differences. The name "protestant," originally referring to the protesting German princes who decreed that each principality had the right to determine its own religious affiliation, became the generic name for the breakaway groups. Today, however, Protestantism thrives in its own right and for many, the term "protest" has never been defined simply in negative terms but has been understood more positively as a "witness" or a statement of belief and practice. At present, there are more than two thousand Protestant groups in the United States alone. The predominant denominations include Lutheran, Episcopalian (Anglican), Methodist, Presbyterian, Church of Christ, and Baptist traditions.

What Protestants Believe

Although they differ among themselves, Protestant belief with few exceptions is premised on a common set of fundamental beliefs.

Justification by faith alone is the belief that human beings cannot do anything to earn their salvation but are redeemed solely by the grace of God. Any good works performed by the believer are thought to be the outcome of salvation, not its precondition. Expressed in these terms, this belief represents Luther's original departure from Catholicism.

Scripture is held to be the primary authority for faith and life. While tradition is important to many Protestants, it is viewed in the light of scripture, history, and an understanding of how the Spirit of God is working through these in the present. From the time of the reformers, the Bible has been translated into vernacular languages so that every member and Christian community has the means as well as the responsibility to read and study it for themselves. Protestant Christians frequently debate the appropriate interpretation of scripture for contemporary ethical and spiritual issues. Conservative congregations apply the words of scripture very literally to belief and practice.

Only two rituals are given the status of *sacraments*. Baptism, by which the individual is sprinkled with or immersed in water, indicates admittance into the church, the family of God. Some traditions baptize infants while others only administer baptism to persons mature enough to make their own statement of faith. The Eucharist, also known as Communion or the Lord's Supper, celebrates the death and resurrection of Jesus. Some Protestants regard the bread and wine of the Eucharist as commemorative symbols, while others believe Christ is really present in the sacrament.

With the phrase, "the priesthood of all believers," Protestants reject the *power of the pope* and by delegation, of the priesthood, believing that all members have direct access to God. Although they have an ordained clergy, the ministers are not celibate nor do they have the same religious authority as the Catholic clergy.

Attitude to Interfaith Marriages

There was a time not very long ago when the marriage of a Methodist to a Presbyterian was considered an interfaith marriage of serious consequence. Over the past few decades, however, an ecumenical movement has brought many Christians closer together. Dialogue and collaboration among Protestants and between Protestants and Catholics have resulted in less suspicion and more cooperation. In effect, the marriage of one Protestant to another of a different Protestant faith, and to a lesser extent to a Catholic, is not as big a departure as marriage to a non-Christian. While no generalization covers all Protestants, the mainline churches tend to be less concerned than many other religious groups over interfaith marriages, but see their role as supportive of the home whatever form that home may take. More recently established denominations, on the other hand, still concerned about their distinctive beliefs and identity, are more resistant to interfaith marriages. Some of these latter groups will not permit their ministers to act as celebrants or their churches to be used as venues for such wedding services. No church, however, refuses to welcome their married believers and non-believing partners and any children those members may have.

Protestant Life

Most churches have a welcoming ceremony for a baby. This may be a baptism, sometimes called a christening, or a baby dedication. It involves a blessing on the child and its family, a challenge to the parents and other church members to raise that child in the faith, and in some cases, the sprinkling of water on the baby's forehead to symbolize her admittance into the church family.

The Sunday School movement was premised on the belief that all believers have the right and obligation to study the Bible for themselves. Originally many Sunday Schools had to begin with lessons in reading and writing, so that the child would be able to read the scriptures. Today, Sunday School classes are held for all age groups beginning with infants and provide a structured curriculum of Bible lessons. Teaching resources and classrooms are set aside by churches for this purpose. As children enter their teen years, the teaching becomes more focused on the study of the specific teachings and practices of the church to prepare them for full membership. The initiation service may be a baptism, if that was not already performed, or a public welcoming ceremony of some kind. Children often have a portion of the main weekly service devoted to them or their own sermon in a room nearby and in some churches they participate as altar boys and girls and choir members. Most denominations run inter-church programs for children and youth that are often a combination of social activity, community service, inspiration, and religious instruction.

Two seasons of the year are especially holy for Christians. The Christmas season, to commemorate the birth of Jesus, is celebrated with special songs, decorations, gift-giving, and nativity re-enactments. Easter recalls the events surrounding the death and resurrection of Christ. Good Friday and Sunday dawn services are a special focus. A period of Lent precedes Easter, in which members are encouraged to make some personal sacrifice as a memorial to the sacrifice of Jesus. After Easter, a period of fifty days marks Pentecost, a time when members recommit to Christian service and witness with prayers for special blessings. Other holy days are marked by different church groups and often the weekly liturgy is built around these themes throughout the year.

Many denominations encourage parents to be religious educators and provide lessons for study at home. The resources are often very well put together with activity suggestions as well as colorful printed materials appropriate for the various age levels. Many homes will offer a prayer at the beginning of meals and teach children to say a bedtime prayer before going to sleep.

Some Protestant denominations run a parochial school system as part of the religious education program. Along with the regular curriculum, children receive instruction in Bible lessons and church practices. Through the church school, children learn to be participants in worship and sometimes are trained as choir members.

In all these provisions for training children, Protestants seek to socialize their children in the faith and by so doing help them find a source of values and guiding principles to sustain them throughout their lives. Belief in God, hope during life's crises, the sense of empowerment to pray directly to God, the ability and right to read and understand the scriptures, and hope in a life to come after death are distinguishing characteristics of a Protestant upbringing.

13

∿∿∿∿∿∿∿∿∿∿∿∿∿∿∿∿∿∿∿∿∿∿∿∿∿∿∿∿∿∿∿∿∿∿∿∿∿

GROWING UP IN OTHER CHRISTIAN FAITHS

E very faith has a variety of forms, whether it be Jewish, Christian, Muslim, Buddhist, or Hindu. Some of these divisions have developed along cultural lines; others along lines of differences in interpretation or practice. This is amply demonstrated by the large number of Christian groups. The representatives of the variety described here all share a common belief in the one God, the power of Jesus to save through his birth, life, death, and resurrection, the Bible as the word of faith, and the call of God to obedience and service. They differ in their understanding of what the Bible means in reference to particular doctrinal beliefs and practices.

Church of Jesus Christ of Latter-day Saints (Mormons)

Mormons draw their sense of identity and history from the *Book of Mormon,* believed to have been inscribed on gold plates that their founder, Joseph Smith, discovered near the place where divine beings visited him. Life centers on the family. Children are regarded as pre-existent spirits waiting to be born and every person carries the potential of moving through the progressive stages of eternity to become increasingly Godlike. God's grace operates primarily within the family unit so eternal marriages and baptisms can be celebrated at a temple for living or dead partners and genealogies are studied for this purpose. Given their focus on the family, Mormons are actively discouraged from marrying outside of their faith. The church provides a strong support system for family worship and religious instruction and daily family worship times are encouraged. The Mormon lifestyle is a reflection of particular family values—pre- or extra-marital sex is forbidden, divorce is discouraged, and drugs including tea, coffee, tobacco, and alcohol are prohibited. Children are prepared for entry into full membership through baptism at about eight years old, and young men must devote two years to evangelistic work. Anybody may attend a Mormon church where laymen preach and the sacrament of the Last Supper is observed, but only Mormon members may enter the temples where rites such as eternal marriages, baptisms for the dead, and endowments (that is, a series of rituals representing the history of salvation) are conducted.

Jehovah's Witnesses

A worldwide movement with over five million members, Jehovah's Witnesses believe that God's kingdom will eventually rule the world and solve the world's problems. For this reason, they actively discourage interfaith marriage, believing that the practice of their faith could be hindered by non-believing partners. Based on their interpretation of the Bible, they do not eat the blood of meat or receive blood transfusions. They do not celebrate Easter or Christmas, because they trace these festivals back to pagan origins, but teach giving to their children as a year-long practice. Putting God's kingdom first in their lives, they are neutral in politics and so do not salute the flag or pledge allegiance to it. In the home, families are encouraged to study the Bible together and aids are published for parents to use. Witnesses do not baptize infants but, valuing individual choice and conscience, baptize by immersion anyone who personally commits to the faith. Baptized members are "witnesses" for God and are known for their house-to-house visits and their periodical, *The Watchtower.* In their meeting places, or "Kingdom Halls," Witnesses hold services up to five times a week, which most members faithfully attend.

Mennonites

Although often regarded as an ethnic group, the Mennonite church is really an international religious movement. Its defining objective is to live plainly and peacefully, so that attention is not distracted from God and doing God's work. Practicing members avoid the accumulation of possessions and wealth, showy clothing, jewelry (including wedding bands) and anything else judged to be merely attention-seeking. Mennonites use money, but reject it as a status symbol and refuse to be debtors. Homes are comfortable but simply furnished. One is likely to find a Bible on the kitchen table, bookshelves filled with religious books, religious pictures on the wall, and decorative religious mottoes scattered about the rooms. Some communities of stricter Mennonites, especially the Amish, press these values further by refusing to have electric appliances and many of the other conveniences associated with modern living. These communities have their own schools and life revolves around the church. Religious instruction and Bible readings are held in the home every morning and evening. All the family attends the weekly church services; children are usually ranged along the front rows while men and women sit on different sides of the center aisle. From birth, families and friends work strenuously to train the child in Mennonite ways of thinking and doing, and even after the age of sixteen, when young people are believed to be mature enough to decide for themselves, the family will continue to pray vigorously that they stay with the church. Young people are baptized at about age eighteen when they are really sure of their decision. A young person who marries outside the church is not shunned, although the Mennonite lifestyle is considered to be the epitome of Christian living. In the stricter communities, if both partners do not join the church, then both must leave. Divorce is forbidden and fighting or squabbling within the home between parents or among siblings is not permitted.

Pentecostals

Named for the period fifty days after the ascension of Christ when the "gifts of the Spirit" were given to the early disciples, Pentecostalism arose in North America in the early days of the twentieth century, although it has assumed a number of different forms since then, including the churches known as Assemblies of God. Worldwide membership in charismatic movements (some within mainstream churches) is estimated to be at least 175 million. Usually conservative in belief and literal in its interpretation of the Bible, Pentecostalism emphasizes the personal experience of the power of God. Family Bible reading and prayer and attendance at services is usually a part of the child's upbringing. Daily devotional guides are published for family worship, which is preferably led by the father, the "priest" of the family. Interfaith marriages are discouraged for the sake of the stability of the home and the faith of the family members. A dedication service for newborns is often performed in which prayers are offered for the child and admonitions given to the family and congregation to do what they can to nurture the child's growing faith. Once a young person has reached the age to make a reasoned decision, he or she can request baptism. A second baptism, that of the Spirit, is usually manifested by physical signs, such as trembling or speaking in tongues. Meetings are often long, involving singing, responses from the congregation, stirring preaching, movement to music, and speaking in tongues. In some congregations, especially during "revivals" with services each day, more spiritual gifts are likely to be demonstrated, including healings. Some Pentecostal congregations support a church school and there are several bible colleges for young people and seminaries to train ministers.

Seventh-day Adventists

Taking both the Old and New Testaments as the foundation for their faith, Seventh-day Adventists worship on Saturday while looking forward to the second coming of Jesus. Missionary minded, they have a worldwide church membership of 3.5 million. Based on the Bible and the interpretations of their founding visionary, Ellen White, Adventists promote a balanced life and have built a comprehensive denominational structure that includes schools and universities, hospitals and health food companies, publishing houses as well as churches. Health-conscious, many members are vegetarians, and alcohol, tobacco, and recreational drug use is actively discouraged. Aids for religious education are provided for all ages. Admission to membership is through baptism for those who can make a reasoned decision and commitment. Given their lifestyle and worship practices (Sabbath is observed as a day free from work and other secular activities from sunset Friday to sunset Saturday) and their commitment to their faith, Adventists discourage marriage with non-believers.

Society of Friends (Quakers)

A pacifist movement which arose in Great Britain during the confusion of the Civil War, the distinguishing Quaker belief is the doctrine of "Inner Light," a reference to the idea of the inner presence of God which, if nurtured and heeded, inevitably leads to truth. At meetings, members will wait in silence until someone has a message from God to share with congregation. Commonly a Quaker marriage to a non-believer is not seen today as an insurmountable difficulty, although a century ago it was often regarded as sufficient cause to "read the member out of meeting." At a couple's request to be married, a Clearness Committee is appointed to see if they are clear to be married, which involves everything from being free of other relationships to knowing how each feels about children and other matters to do with life together. The committee's task is not to see if the couple have made certain prescribed decisions but to ensure that they have addressed and resolved these important issues between them. Once cleared, the couple is appointed a Committee of Oversight that oversees the wedding. A priest does not marry the couple but they marry each other "in the presence of God and these our friends," as the traditional vows put it. In most homes, a silent grace is offered before meals and sometimes the family reads the Bible together. A major principle in child-rearing is to teach the child nonviolence. Children are brought to meetings, but remain with the adults only a little time before going to their own programs. By these means it is hoped that they will learn from the community the method of "speaking from silence." Joining a Quaker congregation is not usually an option until the person has attended for some time. A young person who is old enough to leave home may be invited to join a congregation. If one is interested in making this commitment, a Clearness Committee with functions similar to that for marriage is established to guide the person in the process.

Unitarian Universalists

A combination of two liberal movements, tracing their roots to the free spirits of the Reformation era, Unitarians reject the idea of God as a trinity. Although the movement's roots are in the Judeo-Christian tradition, many members would not regard themselves as Christians, or even as theists. Inclusive in its beliefs, the movement avoids doctrinal tests for membership. Although it has no creed, members subscribe to "seven affirmations" that promote a liberal stand on ethical and social issues. These are summarized as the freedom of religious expression, toleration of religious ideas, acceptance of the authority of reason and conscience, the never-ending search for Truth, the fundamental unity of experience and reality, the worth and dignity of every human being, and the ethical application of religion. Each congregation develops its own programs, but religious instruction and worship experiences tend to draw inspiration from a wide source of religious teachings and practices with some attention paid to the Judeo-Christian along with other world traditions, Unitarian-Universalist history, and social action. It is not uncommon for a member to have experienced Buddhist, Muslim, Christian, Jewish, Native American, and Pagan religious rituals. The inclusiveness of the community is also seen in its acceptance of non-traditional families and ethnic differences. Each member looks to the community for support in finding his or her own way of faith and in providing a religious environment for their children, but packets of materials are made available especially to isolated families. By age fourteen, young people become eligible for membership by receiving instruction and affirming their wish to join. At that time, they "sign the book" of membership in the presence of the minister and another witness.

14

^^

GROWING UP MUSLIM

A Muslim is simply one who submits to the will of Allah, the Arabic name of God Almighty. Islam, the western name for the religion, is built on two primary principles: peace and submission. That is, the Muslim is committed to living in peace with all the created universe of Allah and in submission to the will of Allah. The laws and practices that govern the lives of Muslims are derived from the Qur'an (Koran), the Muslim holy book, and from Al-Hadeeth, the personal sayings of the prophet Muhammad. Although Islam is the most recent world religion, it is currently the world's fastest growing faith, with about one and a half billion followers, nine million of whom live in North America.

What Muslims Believe

Muslims believe in one Supreme God, Allah, the Power that created everything in the universe. Angels are God's creation to convey God's revelations and commandments to humanity and the rest of the universe. The scriptures include the Torah of Moses, the Psalms of David, the Gospels of Jesus, and the Qur'an from the last in this line of prophets, Muhammad. Accepting God's complete authority over human destiny, Muslims look to a Day of Judgment when individuals will be accountable for their actions. Accordingly, life continues after death in either Hell or Heaven.

Islamic beliefs as they are expressed in rituals are summed up in what is commonly known as the "five pillars":

1. *The creed: There is no deity but Allah and Muhammad is His prophet.* Obedience and submission to the laws of Allah give Muslims a sense of sobriety and stability. They reject all other claims to authority, so a Muslim's relationships to others in work, marriage, and politics are seen as contractual arrangements between equals, not in terms of subservience of one to another. So, a Muslim may choose not to stand for the national anthem, take an oath in court, or bow to others, although it is his or her duty to obey the laws of the country if they do not contradict the laws of Allah. While Muslims believe that God has sent the same Islamic message through many prophets—Adam, Noah, Abraham, Moses, Jesus—Muhammad is seen as recalling, completing, finalizing, and completing this message to human beings. Muslims repeat the creed several times a day during daily prayers. If one converts to Islam, he or she is required to repeat this creed in front of two or more witnesses.

2. *Prayer.* Practicing Muslims pray five times a day, whether they are alone or with a congregation and always facing toward Al-Ka'bah, regarded as the first prayer house built for worshiping God in Mecca. Before praying, they will engage at least in a symbolic washing of hands, mouth, nose, face, hair, ears, neck, arms, and feet, although the best ablution is a full shower. The place of prayer is to be clean and dry, and usually a prayer mat is spread on the ground for this purpose. The prayers give worshipers the opportunity to direct their attention to God and reflect on their priorities, sins, commitment, and profession of faith. Friday is a special day for congregational prayer (called *Salaat Al-Jumuah*).

3. *Fasting.* Ramadan, the ninth month of the Islamic lunar calendar, is a twenty-nine or thirty-day period in which Muslims fast from dawn to sunset. During this time they will not eat, drink, smoke, have sex, or disparage others. Fasting focuses the attention on God and believers report that during this month they experience deep changes within themselves and gain a special consciousness of being in God's presence. Muslims remember the needy during this month and give generously to others.

4. *Poor's due.* Muslims believe the poor have the right to share the wealth of the community. They give at least 2½% of their yearly savings to benefit others. Islamic law condemns usury, loans, and interest, because these are ways of making money without working for it and these practices potentially discriminate against the poor. For this reason, many Muslims will not take out a home mortgage or hold interest-bearing savings accounts.

5. *Pilgrimage.* It is the aim and dream of every Muslim to make a pilgrimage to Mecca at least once in a lifetime. The gathering place, the Al-Ka'bah mosque, is believed to have been the original place of worship of God built by Adam and later rebuilt by Abraham and Ishmael. Participation in the pilgrimage is seen as a transforming and unifying experience, commemorating the practices and deeds of Abraham, his wife Hagar, and their son Ishmael.

Attitude to Interfaith Marriages

An underlying Islamic principle is religious freedom. According to the Qur'an, human beings cannot and should not be compelled to accept a particular faith but all have God-given rights to choose their own employment, education, and place and kind of worship, which a Muslim is required to respect and protect.

Preferably, a Muslim man will marry a Muslim woman but is permitted to marry a woman from the "people of the Book" (that is, Jews and Christians) because Islam teaches him to believe in, revere, and accept the majority of their prophets as divinely appointed and to accept their revealed scriptures. He is expected to allow her to pursue her own faith freely and without restraint or coercion. A Muslim woman is permitted to marry only a Muslim man, because it is commonly believed that only with a Muslim husband will she have the freedom to pursue her religious faith as she chooses and because the non-Muslim husband does not accept Muhammad or the teachings of the Qur'an.

It is a Muslim belief that everyone is born by the will of God; that is, everyone is born naturally Muslim, for a Muslim is understood to be simply one who believes in and submits to God in peace. The child of a Muslim man will be brought up in the Muslim faith. When children come of age, they may choose the faith they will commit to.

Muslim Life

At the moment of birth, someone will whisper in the baby's ear the call to prayer and the child's name, in the belief that the bearer of the new name should be the first to hear it. These symbolic acts establish the pattern for the new life— the utter supremacy of God and personal identity through submission to the will of God. Circumcision of baby boys is obligatory following the practice of Muhammad for hygienic purposes and serves as a sign of belonging to the Islamic community. These early rituals are festive occasions for the whole family.

A Muslim home is hospitable, for it is believed guests have rights. A non-Muslim partner may sense this as an intrusion but a visitor may stay for three days before the household may ask about the nature of the visit and negotiate the length of stay. Before entering a Muslim home, it is customary to knock three times and wait for an invitation. Even though the home's resources are shared with guests, privacy is still highly valued. Many remove their shoes before entering because it is also a place of prayer and must remain unpolluted. Intermingling between genders is not free and visitors may not go from room to room, unless permission is given. Before initiating any task, including eating or drinking, a Muslim will repeat the supplication, "In the name of God, the Most Merciful and Most Compassionate." At the end of a meal, a Muslim will say, "Praise God, the Lord of the Universe." Similarly, Muslims repeat the phrase, "Peace and blessing of God be upon him," immediately after naming one of prophets.

In a Muslim home, there is no iconography in the form of statues or paintings to represent the prophets or God, for God is not seen nor approached directly, but Islamic art is nevertheless richly developed. It features geometric patterns and floral designs or beautiful Arabic calligraphy of verses from the Qur'an. A visitor may notice prayer rugs, neatly folded away, ready for use. Light, fresh air, and plenty of flowing water characterize typical Muslim homes for bringing in the outside without exposing the inside; privacy is a principle of Islamic architecture.

At the appointed times, Muslims will pray regardless of where they are, but it is common for the events of the day to be scheduled around prayer times. It is thought best that prayers be made at the mosque, although it is recognized that for women especially, their needs, duties and comforts may make that difficult. When women pray at the mosque, they never bow and prostrate themselves in front of the men for modesty's sake, but will be assigned a place where they have privacy.

Muslims do not gamble, drink alcohol, or eat pork and its by-products. All food is regarded as a gift from God and treated respectfully. Meat has to be slaughtered according to Islamic law. Silver and gold tableware is avoided, and some will eat only with hands in memory of the Prophet's way of life. Similarly, men do not wear gold jewelry or silk clothing, although women may.

The first seven years of life are considered playtime for Muslim children. Little intervention is undertaken to train them in Islamic ways. From about seven years, however, they are taught to take care of their personal hygiene (very important in Islamic practice) and reminded about prayers and the other pillars of Islamic faith. At puberty, the young person is considered accountable to God and assumes the rights and duties of a practicing adult Muslim. While children respect their parents throughout life, at this time they become full participants and equals with their elders.

At this time, the girls will begin wearing the hijab (a full scarf). Muslim dress is designed to afford the greatest modesty and protection. Muslim girls and boys do not wear shorts, swimsuits, or athletic uniforms that break this code, and girls may refuse to be coached by male physical education teachers and sports instructors. While the Muslim faith is gender-free and teaches full equality between men and women, Islamic codes require great respect for women by men. Islam instructs men on how to be sensitive to the sexual and other needs of their wives, while outside of marriage men and women are more socially excluded from each other than they are in western society. Chaperons are present when Muslims of marriageable age meet.

15

GROWING UP HINDU

The vast majority of Hindus live in India, although it is estimated that about 20 million live elsewhere and their numbers in North America and other parts of the western world are growing. As a religion, Hinduism is hard to define, partly because it is difficult to separate the religion from the way of life and partly because Hinduism takes so many different forms depending on geographic location and sectarian and subcultural traditions. As well, it has been said that Indians are capable of living in several centuries at the same time, so elements of traditional Hinduism are mixed in varying proportions with adaptations to modern life.

What Hindus Believe

Some beliefs and practices are fairly common among Hindus, nevertheless. One paradoxical feature of Hinduism is that it is both polytheistic and monotheistic at the same time, unlike the other monotheistic faith traditions already discussed. That is, where Judaism, Christianity, and Islam hold strongly to the idea of one God, Hindus conceive of the Supreme Being as the formless One, but worship it in the form of many gods around whom a complex of stories and myths has been woven. Among the most popular are the trinity of the universe, Brahma, the creator; Vishnu, the preserver; and Shiva, the author of cosmic dissolution. All three Gods have their consorts, who in some ways are even more powerful than their male counterparts, because in the Hindu religion, power and energy are seen as feminine attributes. Since Vishnu is the preserver, he is believed to have undergone nine incarnations, with the tenth to follow, each reappearance coming at a time when he was needed to root out some destructive evil. Krishna and Rama are among the most beloved of these incarnations. Each of the Gods with his respective Goddess, has his own temples, rituals, and festivals.

Hindus pursue four ends or goals in life: *dharma,* or righteous duty; *artha,* or material prosperity; *kaama,* or sensual enjoyment; and *mokshu,* or spiritual liberation. The most fundamental of all Hindu beliefs is the doctrine of *karma,* according to which virtuous deeds are rewarded and wicked actions punished.

Another central tenet of Hinduism is the notion of rebirth. Hindus believe that they pass through many lives. Once they attain *mokshu,* or spiritual liberation, however, they are no longer trapped in the cycle of birth, death, and rebirth. Until then, they will be reborn in higher and lower forms of life, including animal and plant life, depending on their good or bad *karma.* Such a belief engenders reverence for all life forms.

Hindu society is structured hierarchically into four castes, with the *Brahmans,* or priests, at the highest level, followed by the *Kshatriyas* or warriors, *Vaishyas* or merchants, and *Shudras* or peasants and laborers. Outside this fourfold system are the *Panchamas* or fifth class, called "untouchables" because of the menial tasks assigned to them. After India became independent in 1947, untouchability was abolished as unconstitutional. Each caste has its own particular *dharma* or religious obligation, the proper performance of which results in good *karma.*

No single scripture shapes Hindu belief and practice, but a collection of writings known as the Vedas records the revelations that came to wise men and poets of the ancient past. Another collection, the Upanishads, are a commentary on the Vedas made by seers and sages. The Bhagavad Gita is probably the most popular and widely read scripture.

Pilgrimages to sacred sites are common even today. Trees, mountains, caves, and rivers are regarded as holy, the Ganges River being the most sacred of all, and so is lined with temples, shrines, and pilgrim centers. Bathing in rivers is a particularly good thing for a Hindu to do and during festivals or other auspicious days, many will gather for that purpose. When possible, the ashes of the dead are immersed in the waters.

Attitude to Interfaith Marriages

In the traditional view, Hindu marriage is strictly between couples of the same caste, although intercaste marriages do occur. Parents are involved in the selection of partners for their children, in consultation with the family priests, although some allowance is usually made for personal choice. The bride lives with her husband's people as part of an extended family. Marriage to a non-Hindu is an aberration and still not acceptable in strict terms, although old customs are not as powerful as they once were. Hinduism is more flexible in its beliefs and practices than many other religions and less active in seeking converts or making judgments about other faiths, but in traditional families a young person who chooses to marry a westerner may be unwelcome to the family.

The selection of a partner for a traditional Hindu marriage is made with the help of astrological charts prepared for the child by the priests at the time of his or her birth. Charts are also consulted to find the most auspicious day and time for the wedding ceremony. The instructions and advice the priests and parents give to prospective partners have contributed to the relative stability of Hindu marriages in India, where divorce rates are low, but this custom is not working as well in today's increasingly mobile society.

The wedding itself is a large affair, the costs of which are borne by the bride's family. Three is a sacred number, so the rituals may last three days or three hours, or three meals will be served to guests. Fire is a central symbol in Hindu rituals and wedding ceremonies are conducted around one built for the occasion. The priests will chant and pray in Sanskrit. Offerings are made, sometimes in the form of breaking coconuts, or in giving fruit, incense, camphor, or flowers. In some ceremonies, the bride and groom circle the fire seven times, indicating that they intend the relationship to survive through seven rebirths. The bride and groom may take seven steps together on the north side of the fire in the belief that when two persons take seven steps together, they become lifelong friends. In the wedding ceremony, this symbolic rite indicates that friendship is considered the basis of true marriage.

The high point of the ceremony comes when the groom ties the wedding knot joining him and his bride. It is customarily a thread dipped in turmeric and tied around her neck. It could also be a beaded necklace. In either case, it carries two gold pendants, representing marital happiness and well-being. In southern India, this thread is the visible sign of marriage in much the same way as the wedding band is used as a symbol in the West. In the north, this same purpose is served by sprinkling red-colored vermilion powder along the parting in the bride's hair. Rice and flower petals are showered over the heads of the couple by the elders and guests as a blessing at the conclusion of the ceremony.

Hindu Life

A child is brought up Hindu not so much by means of formal religious instruction but by simply being involved in the practices of the faith. Children hear the stories of the gods and accompany their parents to the temples or participate in family devotions at the home shrine and some may learn Sanskrit, the ancient language of Hindu sacred writings. Worship at the temple does not involve sermons or religious teaching but is simply an act of devotion, where the believer prays and offers gifts to the gods. Generally, the practice of Hinduism envelops the growing child and becomes her way of life.

Traditional celebrations mark the birth of a child and sometimes his or her coming of age. A naming ceremony introduces the baby to family and friends. Here the baby's name, usually chosen in honor of a respected ancestor or god, is publicly shared. Sometimes the child's head is shaved or she is anointed in coconut oil and bathed to mark the occasion. Gift-giving and feasting are important elements in the event. Among the upper castes, a further ceremony is performed for boys between the ages of eight and twelve. Known as the thread ceremony, it involves bestowing on him a white string to be worn as a sash throughout his life as a sign that he is required to carry out his religious responsibilities.

While there is no fixed schedule for family visits to a temple for worship, many attend weekly and most on festival days. Prayers are said and offerings are made. Different festival times are appointed for different gods and goddesses or to commemorate various mythic events. In the Festival of Light, for instance, families light lamps around the home which burn all through the night to celebrate Rama's rescue and return of the Goddess, Sita. In some parts of India, Lakshmi, the Goddess of wealth, is worshiped when business people open new accounts.

A Hindu home features art and statuary representing the gods and their stories. Many homes will have an allocated space for devotions, with incense, flowers, coconuts, statues, bowls of red and yellow powder, holy water, lamps, and offerings of various kinds. It is commonly believed that it is good to say God's name as often as possible.

Some older traditional families have a corresponding priest family, which is consulted in marriage matters, keeps the family record of births and deaths, and conducts special ceremonies to observe the many rites of passage. Occasionally, the priest will be invited to conduct a purification or blessing ritual for the home. He will read sacred texts, and offer herbs, sandalwood, and clarified butter in the sacrificial fire.

Hindu society is mostly patriarchal so that power and control are the prerogative of men. More Hindu women today have joined the work force outside the home, which affords them a greater measure of independence, but still, in very traditional homes, the role of women is circumscribed and their domestic duties keep them close to the home.

Hinduism makes a strong effort to cultivate detachment and perform disinterested acts. The accumulation of property and wealth and the forming of close attachments to others are of value only in so far as they are deemed necessary for the good of the family. The ultimate goal is to find a better life in the next rebirth by faithfully fulfilling one's duties in whatever station one now has and finally to attain *moksha*.

16

##

GROWING UP BUDDHIST

The fourth largest religion in the world today, Buddhism arose in India over four centuries before the rise of Christianity and spread first into southeast Asia, then to China, Japan, and Korea, and finally throughout the world. It is difficult to ascertain an exact figure for the number of Buddhists because membership in a particular community is not necessary for the practice of Buddhism; however, it is estimated that there may be over 600 million who identify with the path of the Buddha in some significant way, half a million of whom live in North America.

Developed from the ideas of Siddhartha Gautama, the Buddha, a prince of the royal family of a small kingdom in northern India, Buddhism itself has undergone many changes and given rise to many varieties. Three significant branches are readily identified today: monk-based Theraveda Buddhism; lay oriented Mahayana Buddhism, including Zen Buddhism, which is the best known form of Buddhism in the western world; and Lamaistic Buddhism, which centers around great teachers or Lamas, the best known today being the Dalai Lama.

What Buddhists Believe

Given the range of forms that Buddhism has developed, the differences between various Buddhist practices and beliefs is often greater than their similarities. However, all Buddhists share the life history and teachings of Siddhartha Gautama, believed by many to be the culminating incarnation of many lifetimes of practice as a bodhisattva, that is, one who commits to pursuing enlightenment. As a young and privileged family man, the Buddha confronted "four sights"—a sick person, an old person, a corpse, and an ascetic—which provoked him to make a major change in his life direction. In what is known as the "Going Forth," he left his home and family to seek the meaning of life, especially of suffering and death. Resolving ultimately not to get up from his position under the Bodhi Tree until he had found the solution, he broke through eventually to the realization that, in simplest terms, suffering is produced because of disappointed wants, and therefore, suffering can be avoided when a person ceases to want. The breakthrough to this state of existence, sometimes understood as the realization of the unreality of "self," is one way to describe the enlightenment sought in Buddhist practices. The release from selfish desire and self-centeredness is believed to awaken the universal compassion that the Buddha manifested in his commitment to leading others to achieve the same enlightenment as he.

Buddhism is a religion that does not focus attention on God, and for this reason it is usually regarded as agnostic. Even in those forms of Buddhism that acknowledge "gods," the idea of deities is not central to Buddhist teaching. Instead, its teachings and practices are oriented around personal enlightenment, the experience of knowing the nature and cause of sorrow. All of life is regarded as governed by *karma*, the mystical law of cause and effect, so the creation of good causes leading to enlightenment is the life-shaping goal. Even though Buddha had many disciples during his lifetime, he always insisted that individuals must find out for themselves what is important and pursue their own path toward enlightenment through successive rebirths. Some believe that one who achieves enlightenment will cease to be re-born, entering the state of *nirvana;* others emphasize the ideal of continuing as a bodhisattva within the cycle of life and death to lead others to enlightenment.

Buddhism can be described as a way of living that is balanced and harmonious, not driven by wants or dogged by disappointed striving. Referred to as the Middle Way, it seeks to avoid two extremes—self-denial on the one hand and self-indulgence on the other. This Way is described in terms of eight categories: right belief; right resolve; right speech; right behavior; right occupation; right effort; right concentration; right meditation. It is undergirded by five moral commandments: not to kill or harm any living creature; not to steal; not to lie; not to abuse sex; and not to take intoxicants. Buddhists practice meditation or chanting, commonly focusing on breathing movements, to gain insight into and control over the mental processes. Meditation, in combination with a moral and altruistic way of life, enables the practitioner to transform the desires that cause suffering and to attain enlightenment.

Attitude to Interfaith Marriages
No single rule about interfaith marriages is shared by all Buddhists. Suffice it to say, the forms of Buddhism that are more classically traditional and culture-bound, the more stressful an interfaith marriage would be. There are Buddhists, however, whose egalitarian beliefs about the nature of human beings lead them to see all people as potential Buddhas and who readily accept and learn from others as part of their vision of a united, harmonious humanity. For them, an interfaith family could offer the kind of environment that would promote rather than hinder this basic approach to others.

Buddhist Life

In Theraveda Buddhism, the monks have an active role to play at births, marriages, and funerals. A newborn is taken to the temple where offerings are made, candles are burned, and the baby is given its religious name. At weddings, the monks will chant, burn incense, and offer blessings. In some communities, a string is tied from the statue of Buddha around the couple signifying their common bond and connection with the way of Buddha. Young men in this tradition may choose to live as a monk for at least several months to learn to be separate from the world and all the wants it engenders.

Most Buddhist homes have a shrine, often including a Buddha figure, candles, incense, a bowl of water, and gifts of flowers or fruit. Various forms of Buddhism also include other significant items. For instance, in Soka Gakkai International (translated as the Society for Value Creation), one of the larger lay Buddhist movements in the United States with Japanese roots, a boxed scroll is kept in the shrine. It is decorated with symbols and depictions of various life states—such as tranquility, anger, learning—arranged in a progressive order to remind devotees that they may come in any state of mind and seek to elevate their present life condition. Although brought out during devotions, objects in the shrine are not intended to be worshiped but serve as tools to help focus attention, direct the flow of consciousness, and promote the centering of heart and mind.

Meditation or chanting is often done morning and evening. Whenever possible, this is a family activity. Children are taught more through the example of their parents than through deliberate instruction, reflecting the fact that Buddhism is more a practice than a set of beliefs. Some Buddhist sects publish magazines and other aids for families, but usually the parents are largely on their own in devising religious education for their children.

While some sects have well established communities and temples, most others in the West meet in homes and other buildings not always recognized by outsiders as places of worship. Over time, however, these communities often undertake more elaborate building programs and become more visible in the towns and centers where they meet. It is common for Buddhist communities to meet twice a week to share experiences and communal meditation or chanting. On special occasions or for special causes, a whole day will be devoted to chanting or meditating. Sermons are unusual, for the pursuit of enlightenment is considered a personal quest.

Many are attracted to Buddhism because it seeks harmony among people, between humankind and the environment, and within mind, body, and soul. People are drawn to a state of existence that can help them deal with the stresses of modern life and to the meditation practices and the chanting of mantras that serve as an antidote to the frazzled, materialistic lives that are common today.

17

~~~~~~

GROWING UP WITHOUT RELIGION

Although a great number of religious organizations are to be found in every town, city, and county throughout the country, many people have never stepped inside a church, temple, or mosque. They know very little about the stories, traditions, beliefs, and rituals of the world's religions. Also, many people who would describe themselves as Methodist or Jewish or Catholic attend services and take an active part in religious life only during special seasons, if then. The numbers of inactive members and non-members of religious faiths are so great that our age has been described as the most secular in history.

An atheist is one who rejects the notion that there is a God. Deliberately non-religious, this person may believe that religion is basically a grand deception, devised for people who find life too great a mystery to explain without inventing a supernatural being behind the scenes or else it is promulgated by people who want power and control over others. If they are actively hostile to religion, they may point to the glaring blunders that religious people have made and find their devotional activities ineffectual and meaningless. Talk of God is usually not encouraged in the home and religious motives are looked upon with a measure of suspicion, or possibly skepticism. Learning these attitudes from their parents, children may discredit religious impulses when they confront them. Instead, atheists look to other sources for a sense of meaning and purpose, if they believe such things are to be found in human existence.

Others might be described simply as secular, meaning that they are not concerned with religious matters and live without an articulated sense of the sacred. They go about their daily routines accepting life as it comes. It is common for such families to be so involved in schooling, work, careers, home-building, and socializing with friends that religious concerns simply have no room.

Even so, it would be difficult to identify anybody who did not actually believe at some level that something beyond immediate survival considerations gives value and meaning to life. Although these commitments and values might not always be traditional, they do give shape and direction to the life.

Secular humanism, a label often applied pejoratively by some religious groups to an array of non-religious attitudes, locates the source of goodness and creativity in human beings rather than in something external or supernatural. Seeing goodness and potentially limitless possibilities in humanity, secular humanists promote political and social action programs and attitudes designed to promote human growth. Not all humanists are secular, however, for many religious people share a similar optimism about human nature if it is nurtured in religious faith. Humanists usually encourage in their children attitudes of acceptance of all people regardless of race, gender, sexual orientation, status, or ability. They foster self-esteem, self-reliance, and a sense of self-worth. They provide opportunities for personal development through education and creative projects, while also seeking the improvement of others through charitable work and political action.

Other non-religious people still admit to a belief in God and live by a theology of their own devising, even though they never step inside a traditional place of worship. These "unchurched" might say, for instance, "I believe the Big Guy Upstairs is there when I need him," or, "Sometimes when I look out on the vast distances of space, I see the face of God." A great deal of popular culture expressed in film, novels, and music subscribes to these kinds of religiously flavored ideas and feelings and verifies the fact that spiritual quests are still a part of what human beings engage in to make sense of their lives.

Still others develop a strong spiritual life through alternative means. They may borrow a religious practice as an aid to their private spiritual exercises, such as meditation techniques from an eastern religion or sweat lodge practices from Native Americans. Others commit to a cause such as the environment or a civil rights issue. Still others devote their lives to music or art. They may even introduce their children to a basic understanding of the world's religions. Many of these parents plan experiences for their children that will be profound and memorable. Whether their meaning-making is nurtured and expressed through nature, art, humanistic values, sports, careers, family, voluntary service to others, or patriotism, many people, even some atheists, would regard themselves as spiritual, if not religious.

It is evident, then, that should a religious person join with a non-religious partner their faith will find some common ground although they will certainly have an interfaith home. It is also clear that couples who are not religious *in different ways* may also exhibit the characteristics of an interfaith partnership.

85

Part Three

~~~~~~

MAKING A CHOICE

As an interfaith couple, you have significant options in the religious development of your child. You may choose to bring him up in both faiths, in which case you teach him the beliefs and practices of your respective religions. Or you may opt for no religious upbringing, leaving the choice of faith to the child. Or you may decide to bring him up in one faith—your own, your partner's, or possibly even a third that can serve as a meeting ground for you all. Or one partner may convert so that the home nurtures faith in only one religious tradition. There are advantages and disadvantages with each of these options. In coming to a decision, you need to consider a number of factors, some based in personal commitments, some in your respective religious traditions, some in the larger context of extended family and community, and some in the individual predispositions and choices of the child. Whatever decision is finally made, however, keep in mind that parenting is a matter of teamwork. Just as both parents provide for a child's physical, social, moral, and intellectual development, so they are both needed for his spiritual and religious development, regardless of the particular plan you have made for his religious training.

18

~~~~~~

PARENTING IS TEAMWORK

Before looking at the various options an interfaith couple has in the religious upbringing of the child, it is important to underscore a principle of parenting that applies across all the choices. Good parenting is a team effort. Of course, many single parents successfully raise a child. Many children grow up to be productive, happy, loving adults without the benefit of either mother or father. But, where there are two parents in the home, that home will provide the optimal environment for the child's growth *if* they mutually support each other through all her growing years. Conversely, the key advantage of a two-parent home is jeopardized when parents do not work together—from formulating a plan through carrying it out.

One parent may do the laundry and choose the child's clothes, kiss away the hurt from a scraped knee and teach her how to bake cookies. The other may drive her to school, prepare dinner, and show her how to keep her bike running smoothly. Taking on particular roles like this shares the tasks of parenting while keeping both parents attuned to the child's development. These role delegations, however, are simply ways couples accomplish jointly assumed responsibilities. In the larger picture, both are working cooperatively toward the same ends.

Parents work as a team in the child's education. They both show an interest in her grades and progress at school. One may listen to her early reading attempts and supervise her homework. The other may take time off from work to meet with teachers and accompany her class on field trips. During school vacations, they may join her in enriching and interesting activities. One day, they both will celebrate her graduation. Together, they are contributing to the fulfillment of the overall plan they devised for her learning. This consistent, united team effort provides the security necessary for the child's growth, and ensures that the parents' plans for her education have the best chance for success.

A child's religious upbringing, even in an interfaith home, can and should follow this same model. This, too, is a job for the parent-team. Together, the parents decide which faith or faiths to share with her. They provide the resources, the space, and the time, and give encouragement for making their plan work. And they both do their part in whatever role suits them best to carry their plan forward. One parent may make sure the meals are in keeping with the child's beliefs and special occasions. The other may make sure she gets to meetings on time. Together, they nurture her religious life, helping her to ask questions and look for answers in her personal spiritual quest.

Whatever choice you make for the religious upbringing of your child, she can learn a great deal from an open exposure to the faith of both parents. In *Raising Your Jewish/Christian Child,* Lee Gruzen noted that the adult children of interfaith marriages she interviewed unanimously agreed that it is better to have an easy, comfortable introduction to both faiths than to be raised with no knowledge of one, even when the child's religious training focuses on only the other tradition. Without some knowledge of both faiths, many of these adults reported that they grew up with a sense that they had been denied something important; that they felt cut off from one side of the family; and that they were left with a legacy of cynicism, prejudice, and bitterness rather than of understanding and respect for different others.

Leslie Goodman-Malamuth and Robin Margolis described children's capacity to be touchingly sensitive to the religious loyalties of both parents in their book *Between Two Worlds*. Children know when a parent leaves home to attend temple alone, and more poignantly, at some level, they are attuned to the spiritual exercises, questions, and struggles of those around them. To shelter a child from the faith journey of one of the parents amounts to a loss on the part of both that parent and the child.

In *The Intermarriage Handbook,* Judy Petsonk and Jim Remsen make a significant claim. From their research on interfaith families, they conclude that raising a troubled child is not the inevitable outcome of mixed marriages. Whether children of these homes are raised in one religion, both religions, or no religion has little or no impact on their mental health. The crucial factor is whether or not both parents work together on the same plan. If the parents cannot harmonize their goals, hopes, and strategies for their child's faith development, then the child will suffer. Conversely, we may argue that when parents do work together, the child has a stronger opportunity to develop on the one hand a clear sense of personal identity, and on the other, a reduced feeling of being caught between opposing forces.

Even if the parents jointly decide that their child will be brought up in the faith of only one parent, both of them are fully implicated in that choice. Since both agree to the plan, both are bound to see it carried out as well as they are able.

This may mean that one of you will allow things to come into the home that do not figure in your belief system—a crucifix, a menorah, or a prayer mat. It may mean eating different foods on special occasions—matzoh balls, Christmas cake, or dates to end a fast. It may mean hearing unfamiliar prayers, attending unusual celebrations, helping the child prepare for milestones that you barely recognize—baptism, confirmation, or bat mitzvah. It may mean supporting the young person as she takes up a religiously-oriented career in pastoring, mission-work, rabbinic training, or church school teaching.

In short, a child's religious upbringing should not be the responsibility of only one parent, if both are actively involved in child-raising. You are a religious educator whether or not the child is growing up in your religion. Religious development is encouraged not only through formal support such as taking the child to services and giving her religious lessons at home. It is also encouraged through a cooperative rather than resentful attitude, a willingness to adjust your schedule, and an active interest even as an onlooker and supporter from the sidelines. Sometimes these latter attitudes and informal participations have a very powerful influence, not only on the child's development, but also on the morale and harmony of the home you all share.

19

~~~~~~

OPTION ONE: BRINGING UP A CHILD IN BOTH FAITHS

Joseph and Virginia are thinking about marriage. They met at work and realized as their friendship developed that they had a lot in common and enjoyed each others' company. They have relatively secure jobs and bright futures and both are ready to settle down and look forward to having children and raising a family. Their biggest hurdle is that Joseph is Jewish and Virginia is Christian. And for both, their religion is an important factor in their lives. If truth be known, they are drawn to each other in part because they share a mutual interest in spiritual things and in part because there is a sense of the exotic, adventure, and risk-taking that comes with stepping out of one's own tradition.

In their friendship and courtship, neither Joseph nor Virginia feel compelled to change their religious life. Joseph continues to attend services often on Friday evening and most Saturday mornings and works in a program for Jewish young people. Virginia enjoys the Sabbath evening service at his parent's home when they visit together. She regularly attends Sunday morning services where she sings in the choir and teaches Sunday School. She also has choir practice for an hour on Friday evening. Joseph enjoys the Christmas traditions Virginia's family observe.

Because their respective religions are important to them both, they have decided to raise any children they might have in both faiths. They are drawn to this solution for a number of very good reasons.

- Both feel they have much to share with a son or daughter that is good and helpful. They value their own upbringing and the opportunities they had for growing spiritually. Neither wants the child to be ignorant of the faith that gives them hope, identity, and community.
- They feel more confident about contributing to a child's spiritual development in the religious terms with which they are most familiar. Joseph knows and values Judaism—he was brought up with the words of the Torah; Virginia knows and cherishes Christianity—her earliest memories are of entering the sanctuary, hearing the choir, and watching the candles being lit. They each believe their way of faith is right and true for them.
- Virginia and Joseph plan to be parents very much involved in raising any children they might have. Both imagine how wonderful it will be to do things together, like going to church or preparing for a bar or bat mitzvah.
- The couple knows that their respective parents and siblings not only will urge that their child be brought up in their own particular family faith but will eagerly take on the role of godparents and sponsors. The child will have a wonderful support system from both families.
- They see a unique opportunity to teach their child about the kinds of differences that make up our world, especially how to appreciate and accept religious differences.

In choosing to go with both faiths, however, Virginia and Joseph are pondering a number of important questions:

• In the development of faith, the deep motives of heart and soul are called into play. Values, beliefs, and practices make up the religious life. There is much to learn, a great deal of time and energy is spent, commitments are encouraged, and duties are prescribed. Is it possible to give so much to two traditions? By attempting to impart two faiths, could they end up teaching neither well?

• If this approach to religious upbringing does not encourage a full commitment to either religion because another set of religious beliefs and practices is always present, will the child really have the benefit of all that a religion can offer?

• How much religion does a child need in the course of a normal week? Could they be overdoing religious training by placing two sets of religious demands on their child?

• What will they do about the inevitable disagreements that arise between two religions? How can they teach their child that Christianity is right and Judaism is right when the two religions don't agree on important things like the proper day for worship, or what makes up scripture, or who God is, or how God should be worshiped? Will they simply be confusing the child to the extent that he will not want anything to do with religion at all, or worse, grow up without a clear sense of commitment or of who he really is?

• Is there a way that both faiths can be shared with their child that will maximize the benefits and go some way toward answering these doubts?

Some suggestions for putting this last approach into practice are offered in the next Key.

20

PUTTING OPTION
ONE INTO
PRACTICE

Some might be tempted to think that when Virginia and Joseph decided to bring their child up in two religious traditions they would avoid having to compromise. After all, neither religion is preferred over the other; neither parent has to give up passing on his or her faith to the child. But in practice, compromise becomes a daily challenge when two faiths operate together. Joseph and Virginia will have to find a meeting of minds over many issues along the way. Will they arrange a *brit milah* (circumcision ritual) for their son when he is eight days old, a christening service for their newborn, or both? Will they name their child Daniel or Paul, Rebekah or Mary? Will they attend Passover or Easter services that fall on the same weekend, or create some combination of both? Will they pray with heads covered to Hashem or in the name of Jesus? Will their child be initiated through bar mitzvah into the Jewish faith or baptized as a Christian? Will they send him to a Jewish day school, a Christian school, or a public school? Give and take will be required of both parents as they seek to make choices.

In particular they will need to:

* *Create a reasonable schedule.*
   Attending all the offerings of both congregations may quickly prove unworkable. Virginia and Joseph are wondering wheth-

er they will take their child to their respective services every other week, while making sure that he would not miss high services in either community so they would be in church for Easter and Christmas and at temple for Rosh Hashanah and Passover. Religious instruction and rituals at home, such as saying grace before meals and welcoming in the Sabbath, having a Christmas tree and lighting Hanukkah candles, observing Lent and having a kosher kitchen, would also need to be arranged. Before too long, they will realize that a schedule that tries to accomplish everything will not be sustainable. If they are like other similar families, either the child will accompany one parent most of the time, or he will only accompany each parent on special occasions.

• *Figure out beforehand how you will answer his religious questions.*
Sooner or later the child is going to ask why Daddy isn't coming to church or why Mommy isn't in temple. He may ask who God is or other questions that would be answered differently by each parent. His parents can use these opportunities to explain their common ground and their differences. They can say, "Both Mommy and Daddy like going to services; it's just that we go to different services because we go to the one we prefer," or, "We go to the same one as Grandma and Grandpa," or, "We go to one we have gone to all our lives" or something similar. Or, "Mommy and Daddy believe that God is the one who made us and cares for us and tells us how to do the right thing. Mommy also believes that God sent his Son to live with people to show them who he is." These answers both confirm the other partner and acknowledge legitimate differences. As children grow older, they will probably want to probe these answers further, in which case, Virginia and Joseph should give honest answers without insisting that the other is wrong. Children can handle differences honestly acknowledged better than all-out conflict.

At some point, the child is probably going to ask what religion he is. Parents should be positive in their answer. They can say something like, "You are very lucky because you have two religions in your family and you can be both." If they have the opportunity to explore this further, they might ask him what he enjoys about both religions, what he finds good about having two religions in the home, and what religion or mixture of religion he would like to be. These kinds of follow-up conversations will strengthen his sense of who he is and empower him to create his own religious identity.

Some interfaith couples report that their child was terrified when he first learned about the Holocaust and wanted to know whether he or one of his parents was going to be killed for being Jewish. This kind of episode can give parents a wonderful opportunity to talk about the benefits of their interfaith home—a place where different people learn to understand and love each other so that such terrible things as Holocausts never happen again.

- *Adjust to the changing needs of the growing child.*
In the child's earliest years, it is relatively easy for parents to work out a schedule that gives both religions appropriate time and significance. What Joseph and Virginia must realize, however, is that as a child grows, he will develop preferences and interests independent sometimes of what they might plan. His best friends may belong to the Christian children's club, for instance, so he will want to attend there, but he prefers the Jewish religious instruction workbook he has been using at home. They should anticipate that they all will have adjustments like this to make along the way in line with his needs and preferences. Being prepared for them will help make transitions as smooth as possible.

While the plan is to keep the balance between faiths as long as possible, there may and probably will come a time when their child, reared in both faiths, will be increasingly drawn to one faith over the other or decide against both. Parents' inability to predict their child's choices should be compensated for by a measure of freedom for him to develop those preferences.

• *Develop a strategy for resolving conflicts.*
Compromise is an art, but there are specific steps Virginia and Joseph can take. First, they must maintain an ongoing assessment of how things are working out, *sharing* with each other and being *honest* when they observe a spiritual change or development that makes them feel glad or upset or irritated at the way their plan is working out in practice. As their child grows, he may join in on these discussions.

Second, once a conflict is identified, together they should focus on *really hearing each other* on the matter, realizing that it is taken with some seriousness by at least one of them. They need to be careful not to think that what they believe and see is what their partner or child believes and sees.

Third, since problems are opportunities for creative solutions, they can look for an answer together, determining what's *fair*, whether there is *a better way* of going about things, how the *child is best served,* and what is *workable.*

Fourth, they should *wholeheartedly* try their solution, keeping an open mind on how to make ongoing compromise work.

• *Expect some irreconcilable differences.*
At times there will be no logical solution. The child simply cannot be taught at the same time that the Messiah is yet to come and that Jesus is the Messiah; that Saturday is the proper day of worship and that Sunday is; that Torah is God's word and that the Old and New Testaments together are God's word. In finding compromise here, Virginia and Joseph have a number of possibilities:

— One view or the other may prevail. One parent will agree not to press for his or her belief for the sake of simplifying what they teach their child.

— Both views can be moderated. They may choose to teach, for instance, that Jesus is the Messiah in Christianity but not in Judaism; both Saturday and Sunday are days for worship; God's voice is heard in the Torah and throughout the Christian Bible.

— They may allow both views to remain on the table, to be resolved one way or another by each family member individually.

Just as no couple will agree on everything—even on what color to paint the living room walls and where to go for this year's vacation—so they may agree to disagree on some matters of faith. Children do not always need to be kept from knowing about their parents' disagreements, although no family should resort to a screaming match to resolve them. A measure of large-heartedness and respect for each other's loyalties will help them all maintain harmony in the home and personal integrity in what they choose to believe.

21

∧∧∧

OPTION TWO: BRINGING UP A CHILD IN NEITHER FAITH

Jason occasionally attends synagogue with his parents, his sister, and her family. He enjoys the sense of belonging to a community of Jews and, having grown up in this congregation, feels very much at home with these people. They have known him from birth, watched him grow into manhood, attended his bar mitzvah, and still attempt to get him involved in working with the university's Jewish students' association. He would like to go to Israel someday and follows events there in newspapers and magazines his family passes on to him. His work as an administrator at the local campus of the state university has brought him into contact with scholars in Jewish studies and in other branches of religious studies. He usually has a weekly lunch with his good conversation partner, the professor of East Asian studies, and through him has learned considerably more about Buddhist, Taoist, and other expressions of faith.

Jason's fiancée, Robin, is a professor of history, with a special interest in the history of the western, Christian world. Although she is critical of much that has been done in the name of Christianity, she would not miss going to church at Easter, for it is a family tradition to attend both the sunrise and the mid-morning services and then have a family reunion lunch at her parents' home. She loves the Christmas season, except for what she considers its crass commercialism, and finds the Christmas Eve services very moving. Sometimes she just needs to go to church to be in touch with her spiritual life through the hymns, prayers, and sermons of communal worship.

During their courtship, both have maintained their connections with their usual traditions, although neither one has attended any services with the other. In their leisure time they enjoy the theater and both are members of the university faculty orchestra. In their love of music they find a great deal of inspiration, although they are both only amateur performers.

The question they wrestle with is: What religious upbringing will we give our child if and when we decide to have a family? At present, they have decided to let any child of theirs grow up without involvement in religion, either Judaism or Christianity, or, as far as they are concerned, any other faith, because they do not know another religion well enough to pass it on. What kinds of considerations brought them to this decision?

- Both Jason and Robin have been connected with a particular religious community all their lives, but neither of them regard these communities as indispensable. In a sense, they feel they were born into the religion of their parents and it had become habitual to attend but not essential for their spiritual development. Neither feel compelled to pass their particular faith on to their children.
- In the diverse world of today and in the multifaith family they are about to become, they fear that religious differences can

be divisive. They imagine they could very easily end up disagreeing over which religion should prevail in the home or squabbling over which religion was not being given a fair hearing. Better, they argue, to do their own thing individually with the traditions they have been brought up in, but leave their child out of it.

- One thing they both regret is that they simply accepted the religion they had been born into and without question remain with. They had not examined other possibilities but had simply let circumstances decide their religious affiliation for them. Rather than decide for their child, they would prefer that she make up her own mind. She would see her dad attending Jewish events and her mom participating in the Episcopal church. She would be free, they agree, to accept either or neither religious faith—they will not coerce her in any way.

- They believe they have many other ways to encourage their child's spiritual development. They will involve her in music and art and theater, and put her in touch with her spiritual self by sharing the beauties of the natural world with her and giving her opportunities to do something for others. She will not grow up without a sense of God, they argue, but without the baggage that religion can sometimes carry.

- They agree not to prevent their child from accompanying either one of them to services or special events or even from joining their particular congregation at some time if she so chooses.

Robin and Jason know they are not alone in deciding against deliberately working to pass on their religious faiths to their children. In fact, their families will probably not offer overwhelming resistance to this decision, except for an occasional aunt here or grandparent there, for although both sides would prefer to see the child raised in their particular faith, they accept it as commonplace now for people to leave the family religion. They would like to see the child in church or synagogue, of course, but as long as she has a good home and caring parents, they will settle for that. The couple, however, do carry some doubts with them.

- Robin wonders sometimes how nice it would be if the children were with her and her family on Easter Sunday at the services and then later for lunch with the family. Of course, Jason and the kids could come for lunch only, but something would be missing if they hadn't been there all along. Jason knows he would not be able to watch as other girls celebrated their bat mitzvah without some sorrow that his own child would not. He knows that when he feels an occasional pang of nostalgia for his Jewish roots he also knows that his own child might not have the same sense of heritage. Yes, there will be some regrets.
- More than that, will their family cohere as a unit when mother and father and child go their separate ways for spiritual nurture? They could sense a lack of togetherness in something as significant as faith.
- Could they really manage spiritual nurture without the support of a community of people who are used to doing this and have the resources and experience to do it well? They suspect they will be groping in unknown and uncharted territory trying to accomplish this task independently.
- What if the child grows up to accept wholeheartedly the religion of one parent? Would the other parent feel alone? Would that parent feel a sense of failure or betrayal? Would they feel comfortable with the child's choice?

Following are some guidelines that might be useful in carrying out this option of not bringing the child up in the faith of either parent. They may go some way toward addressing these doubts.

22

PUTTING OPTION TWO INTO PRACTICE

Jason and Robin's choice to bring their child up without involving her in the religion of either might be construed as failing to make a positive choice. They each have something—a tradition, a community of faith, a set of beliefs, practices, and emotional involvements—but are planning to live their lives with each other and their children without sharing these things with them. Have they really resolved their interfaith differences or only put them to one side? More than this, can they carry their plan through, as the years go by and pressures from various quarters have to be dealt with?

Robin knows that when their child begins school, Grandma will want to give her a copy of the Children's Bible as she has done for all the other grandchildren. She also knows that the minister from her church will approach them to schedule a series of pastoral visits once they set up their new home. Jason knows how disappointed his family and congregation will be if they do not have the usual ceremonies for welcoming a new Jewish baby, and how difficult it will be for their child later when she sees all the fuss the family makes over the cousins who are preparing for bar mitzvah. There will be pressures in one form or another and even some criticism from both sides of the family, they suspect. If they think ahead imaginatively, they will also be able to picture their child coming to them with questions, curiosity, preferences, choices, and frankly, the knack of knowing how to play one parent off against the other. To be workable, their plan needs to be undergirded with several understandings.

- *Agree to share the plan with those who need to know.*
The family, friends, and congregation who are likely to interact with their child will be able to cooperate best if they know what plans Jason and Robin have formulated. Better to make their position clear from the beginning than to have to deal with incident by incident as they occur. As the child grows, they can explain it to her, too, so she understands what is happening and why, and can feel free to ask questions and join in with the religious happenings around her as she wishes. She can also be empowered to know how best to respond when pressured by others to go one way or the other. When Grandma's Bible arrives, Jason and Robin might sit down with their daughter and look at it together, even read some of the stories from it, while explaining that this is Grandma's special holy book. By their demeanor, they can affirm Grandma in the child's eyes, without either endorsing her particular religious tradition or denouncing it. Overall, they should be consistent and firm in their decision, knowing they believe it to be best for their child.
- *Agree on how much exposure the child will have to each religion.*
While their intention is not to bring her up deliberately to be a fully committed member of either faith, it is unrealistic, and probably undesirable, for their child to know nothing of her parents' religions. But how much exposure shall they give her? This question is difficult in the abstract, but if they were to imagine possible scenarios, they might be able to agree on how to handle them. They could ask:

— What will they do to mark the birth of their baby? Can they create their own celebration or shall they choose one or the other usual celebrations of their respective traditions?

— What will they record as their child's religion if it is required on any official form?

— What would they do if the congregation was having a special event for children?

— How often should they take her to services with them?

— How will they prepare her for her cousin's bat mitzvah celebration?

— What shall they do about Christmas dinner and gift buying, especially if they go to the family dinner on Christmas day?

— How will they respond to requests from friends or family members who offer to take the child to some religious event they believe she will enjoy?

— How will they answer those inevitable questions about who God is, and what happens when we die, and why do bad things happen? What will they say when their child wants to know what religion she is?

As a general rule, it is best to allow her to become acquainted with a variety of religious beliefs and practices with tolerance and understanding. Give her as much exposure as she seems to be interested in, while always attempting to treat both (all) religions fairly.

• *Agree on a plan for nurturing her spiritual development.*

Parents who have a religious community usually have the resources and expertise of that community to call on as they seek to instill values, and promote moral behavior and a sense of reverence or awe or worship in their children. Jason and Robin will face the same challenges as any parent, and will need to devote the same care and attention, time and energy, and personal involvement with her so that she will grow strong in soul as well as body and mind. The difference is that they will largely be on their own in this. So they will need to devise ways of promoting her personal spiritual growth. Like all parents, and perhaps more than many, they will need to look for good books, talk with her about the wonders of a sunset and a growing plant, find occasions both regular and informal to bring up the big questions about the meaning of things, and who we are, and why we are here, and what we should do. In other words, they should take seriously their responsibility as spiritual educators, whether or not this task is undertaken within a particular religious tradition.

• *Agree on how to respond to her religious interests.*
While the parents will be able to establish parameters for maintaining neutral ground, the child may have her own ideas about what she wants to do about religion. How will they respond if she wants to learn Hebrew or attend Sunday School, refuse to eat pork like her dad or want to wear a crucifix like her mom, take part in the Christmas pageant or be in synagogue for Yom Kippur? They should keep in mind that interests like this may be more than religious. They may be driven by a desire to be with her friends or to do what they are doing so she doesn't feel different. They may be an outworking of her relationship with her parents, for good or ill. In any case, they can treat these requests with respect, discuss them together as a family, and hesitate to pass judgment on them. In the end, it is usually best if they support her choices, even though they suspect these may be only whims. By doing so they will demonstrate that they are giving her some measure of freedom in finding her own religious pathway.

23

▲▲▲

OPTION THREE: BRINGING UP A CHILD IN ONE FAITH

When she graduated, Carla took an appointment in Saudi Arabia with a volunteer organization. Her parents were glad that she was taking this opportunity to experience another part of the world, but they were a little apprehensive about her traveling so far from home. Carla, however, loved the place from the moment she arrived. Quiet and sensitive, she nevertheless made friends easily and was soon involved in outings and events with other volunteers as well as young people from the local area. After a furlough home, she signed up for another stint with the same organization.

It was during this second contract that her parents received a letter from her announcing her plans to marry a man she had met in Saudi, Isma'il. They would return to the United States for the wedding and remain several years while Isma'il completed his university studies. If her parents had mixed feelings about her going to Saudi in the first place, this news was greeted with an even greater measure of joy and misgiving. When they met Isma'il and saw the two of them together, they appeared happy, but they were still concerned about the matter of cultural and religious differences, for Isma'il was Muslim and Carla had been brought up Christian.

The couple had of course already talked about these differences. Christianity and Islam support many of the same values and moral behaviors, worship the same God, and share a great deal of common heritage; however, there is still an enormous gap between the two faiths. Together, Carla and Isma'il had agreed to bring their child up as a Muslim. They came to this agreement for a number of reasons:

• Since they planned to return to the Middle East when Isma'il's studies were done, they considered it appropriate to raise their child in the prevailing religious culture. This way, they would have the support of family, friends, and the wider community and he would fit more easily into the local milieu.

• They knew that the expectations on Isma'il to bring his child up Muslim were very strong. While Carla would be free to remain Christian, there would be constant pressure and the force of tradition for their child to follow his father's faith. Carla's parents would probably send gifts with a Christian flavor and make a big deal of Christmas. The couple agreed that this acquaintance with Christianity would be a good educational experience for him, while predicting that the Muslim influence on their home and lifestyle would be stronger.

• Although Carla would not change her faith, she had developed a deep appreciation for the Muslim way of life and beliefs. She had come to know Isma'il's family and was accepted by most of them. She sometimes joined them at the mosque, although she did not participate in their prayers. Often she took care of the children while their mothers worshipped. She felt at home with their practices and believed she would not be uncomfortable with her child participating in them.

Isma'il and Carla also knew that their decision would not be as uncomplicated as it sounded and that there would be implications they would have to deal with along the way.

• Would Carla always be content to see her children involved in a faith and culture that she might appreciate but would never be able to embrace fully? Would she increasingly feel an outsider in her own family, as her husband and children shared so much among themselves and with others of which she would not be a part?

• What would they do if their plans changed and they were to remain in the United States instead of returning to Saudi or they were to take up permanent residency in the States sometime in the future? Being Muslim in a predominantly Judeo-Christian society might bring its own problems for their child, but then so would changing the child's religious orientation to fit in with the culture they happened to be living in at a particular time.

• How would they respond to any interests their child might show in Christianity? Would they actively discourage him, try to put off acting on these interests until he was older, or let him decide for himself as soon as he wanted to, even though it might mean revising their original plan?

• If the worst should happen and their marriage break down at some point in the future, what would be the conditions for a divorce? Was divorce permissible in this faith tradition? Should they separate, had Carla surrendered or jeopardized her rights to the children by bringing them up in their father's faith?

While their case has some unique features, many of these same reasons and concerns appear in one form or another for other interfaith couples who prefer to focus on raising their child in one religion. The following Key offers some suggestions that might facilitate this particular choice.

24

PUTTING OPTION THREE INTO PRACTICE

Isma'il and Carla's decision to bring up their child in the faith of one parent, in this case the father's, may seem to be the most logical decision. As their plans presently stand, they will be immersed in his culture and religion by returning to the Middle East and Carla already values his religion. Furthermore, knowing the Muslim people as well as she does, she has obviously come to appreciate how important Isma'il's commitment is to bringing up his children in his faith. Not all interfaith marriages have such a clear cut choice as this appears. Many times, negotiations are more stressful and consensus is difficult to find. Sometimes, families and friends on both sides exert pressures and the pull of the faith traditions of both of the partners are more or less equally powerful, making the choice between them more difficult.

Many parents decide not to divide their child's loyalties and attention by trying to expose him to two religions, nor do they want to deprive him of the opportunity to discover fully all that any religion can offer by ignoring or avoiding religion altogether. For them, the best option may be to raise him in the faith of one of them. But how can they choose the right faith?

- *Share your reasoning with your partner.*

  This would seem to be so apparent it hardly needs mentioning, but a common mistake newlyweds and about-to-be-weds make is to imagine they will be able to change their partner after they are married. This is usually a false hope and not an honest or fair way to begin a lifetime together. It's better to get all your thinking about this issue out in the open early to avoid misunderstanding or disappointment later. If you would really like your child to be reared in your faith, say so up front. If you believe your partner's faith is more appropriate, say that, and give your reasons. Without this honesty and openness from the beginning, you cannot arrive at a genuine consensus and could be in for some unwanted surprises later.

- *Hear your partner.*

  As you are willing to share what is on your mind about your child's upbringing, so accept that your partner also has things to share. It is one thing to listen and another thing to really hear. Let her say all that she has to say, ask questions when she is done, not in an effort to undermine her stand, but to help you understand it better—so keep sarcasm, irony, teasing, and belittling tones out of your discussion altogether. When both of you have had an opportunity to share what you are thinking—and this may take days, months, or even years—and you know you have been heard, then an agreement can begin to evolve.

- *Choose the faith that best fits.*

  Since faith is a way of life and not something tacked on to everyday living for special events, consider your lifestyle and the dreams you have for your child's early life, and imagine how both faiths could work. Which seems better supported by the living environment you envision for your home? What community of believers is most accessible, most relevant, and most appealing to a young person growing up? Which faith could your combined efforts most readily be directed toward? How can you best provide a religious education for him?

Choosing a faith for the child is only the first step. As you become increasingly comfortable with your choice, another set of decisions will need to be made to flesh out how you will put that choice into practice.

- *Decide on a level of involvement for your child.*
Given that you are or will be a multifaith family choosing to focus your child's attention on one religion, will you want him to participate in everything or only part of what that faith community has to offer—including attending services, enrolling in the religious day school, preparing for full membership in that community, strictly adopting the customs, habits, rituals, and beliefs of that community, and so on? In general, once parents have made a choice, then it follows that commitment to that faith should be wholehearted and consistent. Religious training—and this entails using all the means at your disposal, with every intention of being thorough and careful—not done well can be more deleterious on your child's personal development than no religious training at all.

However, between yourselves you may consider some compromises that make your choice more comfortable for both partners. For instance, you may choose to send your child to a public school instead of a religious school, or you will encourage him to join the boy scouts instead of the local church children's group.

- *Decide on your level of involvement.*
Obviously when one faith is chosen over another in an interfaith household, the parent whose religion has been chosen

will carry considerable responsibility. She knows the faith and its traditions best and also probably the religious education opportunities that the community offers. However, the other parent also has a role to play in the spiritual and religious development of the child. Will he attend services often, seldom, or never? Will he supervise prayers? Will he celebrate the special seasons with them? Will he encourage and support them as they prepare to become full members in their faith community? As a general rule, his support and willingness to be a partner in the child's religious education, where it does not compromise his own faith, strengthens the bonds among family members and becomes a living example of the pleasures and benefits that come from being part of a multifaith world. One thing this partner should decide is not to undermine his spouse's efforts by being uncooperative, by ridiculing, or by constantly tempting the child away from the chosen faith with other appealing but conflicting activities.

While one faith is the center of a child's attention, however, he should not be ignorant of the spiritual journey of both parents. They might celebrate some of these unfamiliar rituals or take the child to services to acquaint him with that community, and, especially, share the stories from this other tradition. That way, he is less likely to feel cut off from a significant part of both parents' lives and families and from a tradition that is also part of his heritage.

25

▲▲▲

DECIDING FACTORS

F rom reading through the previous Keys it should by now be quite apparent that there is no simple solution to dealing with religious differences in a multifaith family. No one decision is appropriate for all families because every family is made up of a unique collection of histories, internal and external dynamics, and personalities. Pros and cons of the various options need to be identified and weighed in the light of your family's particular circumstances.

While the preceding Keys have identified three main options for your consideration, variations on these choices are also possible and are sometimes demanded by the situation in which you find yourself. You may decide, for instance, to share both faiths with your child, but not during the same years. Or you may share one faith with your firstborn and another with the second child. Or you may decide to have your child involved in one faith at a relatively low level until she is old enough to decide what to do about religion in her life. From questionnaires they received from 185 adult children of Jewish-Christian interfaith families, Leslie Goodman-Malamuth and Robin Margolis found that 17% had been raised as Jews, 41% as Christians (including Quakers and Unitarians), 19% with exposure (slight or significant) to both faiths; and 23% in a third, "compromise" faith or no particular faith at all (*Between Two Worlds*). In your discussions together as parents-to-be, think of your own situation specifically and creatively work to find your best solution.

Although the possible choices vary widely, from imparting no religion, to bringing the child up in one religion, to finding a way of teaching both religions, the same kind of factors need to be considered as you formulate your plans for your child's religious upbringing. Here is a checklist, by way of a summary, of some of the key questions to ask yourself as you work your way toward a decision:

- How important to each of us is our own religious faith?
- What do I find indispensable in my own faith practices and beliefs?
- What do I find of value in my partner's faith?
- What do I disparage in my partner's faith?
- How well do I tolerate differences, especially when they are right in my home?
- Will I be happy allowing my partner to follow his religious journey even though it may be different from my own?
- What is the prevailing religious/cultural environment of our neighborhood, town, and country?
- What resources do our respective faith communities have to bolster the religious training we will give in the home?
- What support network of family and friends do we each have for raising our child in our faiths?
- How cooperative will our family and friends be with our plan for our child's religious upbringing?
- Am I honest about expressing my own views without being dogmatic on the one hand or reticent to say what I really feel on the other hand?
- Can I listen and actually hear what my partner is saying?
- Do I feel threatened when I don't get my own way, or can I see the larger picture of two people working together for the good of their child?
- Can I remain reasonable and open throughout our discussions, or do I become so emotionally involved I am difficult to negotiate with?

- How involved do each of us want to be in our child's religious formation?
- How involved in religion do we want our child to be?
- How comfortable will I be carrying the major responsibility of sharing my faith with my child?
- How comfortable will I be if my partner shares her faith with our child?
- What am I willing to contribute to our child's religious development in a faith different from my own?
- Will I feel shut out of my child's life if she doesn't share my religion with me?
- Am I consistent when a decision is made or will I always want to reconsider it?
- How much freedom to choose her religion will I be willing to give our child?

This is not an exhaustive list of questions to ask, again because each family has its own unique situation, but hopefully it will prompt you to ask the kind of questions of yourselves as individuals and as a couple that must be addressed if you are to find your own workable solution. Permeating this list are three major characteristics you can bring to the negotiations:

Honesty. Be open, true, and believable—then you will have a trustworthy foundation on which to negotiate.

Care. Take time to know your own heart and to hear your partner's needs and desires—then your choices will promote the well-being of you all, parents and child.

Fairness. Consider all sides of the discussion and all possibilities to find what will best accommodate your needs, your partner's, and your child's—then you will have made a choice that will hold fast in the long term.

26

‸‸

A CHILD'S POWER OF CHOICE

U p to this point, the focus has been on the parents in an interfaith home. What are their religious commitments and what aspirations do they have for their child? What are the potential problems and possibilities for an interfaith family? What options for their child's religious upbringing do they have and how shall they choose among them? This attention is justified, because the first decisions to be made do lie with the parents. Their choices and actions demand a great deal of careful thought for they will influence the child throughout his life.

Indirectly, however, the real focus of attention has been on the child, for it is his welfare, his experience of religion, his spiritual development, and his faith commitment that the discussion has really been about. Our purpose all along has been to find a way of dealing with religious differences between the parents with the child's interests in mind. From the start and all the way through, your plans should evolve along the lines of what you believe to be best for him.

How can you know what is best for the child? You know your own dreams and aspirations can get in the way of your objectivity. The child's immaturity can convince you that you can always make better choices than he can. But through all these distractions, you need to see his interests and needs and

117

hear his preferences as he matures into a self-determining adult. One of the greatest gifts a couple can give for their child's religious development is an environment that encourages his growing power to choose.

Religious freedom is clearly more than a constitutional amendment. The right to choose which faith to follow and to have the freedom to pursue that faith in belief and practice makes not only for a democratic and more harmonious nation; it is the essence of religion itself. Forced religion is diminished and corrupted religion. No path of genuine faith is occupied by believers who have had no choice about whether they follow it or not. If an interfaith home is founded on religious freedom, then good things follow. Respect for diversity, independent decision-making, room for personal growth, and an atmosphere less charged with criticism and judgmental attitudes are promoted.

A child, however, is not born with the full-blown ability to exercise religious freedom wisely. It is something he learns through practice and education. But it is a training that should not be left until the child has reached his teen years. Rather it is something that he gradually grows into, adding skill and wisdom as he goes. Here are some practical steps to guide you in this process as it applies to a child's religious upbringing through his various stages of development.

From a young age, give the child the opportunity to make some choices within the religious boundaries you have set for him. Which Bible story would he like to hear tonight? Which prayer mat will he use? Will he light the candle or hold the book of readings? Stand by his decisions so that they are known to be genuine choices. If your child should ask why your spouse doesn't come to services with you, for instance, you might suggest that he has different ideas. Avoid implying that these ideas are bad or wrong. Be prepared to follow up by describing in simple terms how they are different.

As the child grows, the simple choices can be replaced with more significant ones. In elementary school you might ask him, Does he want to join the children's club? Does he want to be a part of the Christmas pageant, or sing in the children's choir? Will we all go to Easter services this year or Passover? Will we go to our Passover service, but also attend the dawn Easter service with Mom this year as well?

Answer his questions as honestly as you can. Why is Mommy not coming to church with us? Why are we always going to the mosque? Why do I have to go to the Christian school as well as learn Hebrew? Why do I have to wear a yarmulke and Dad doesn't? The most difficult questions to answer are those that call for judgments of your partner's faith or that give a negative impression of it. Will Daddy go to hell if he doesn't come to church with us? Mom doesn't believe the Qur'an—is that bad? Dad doesn't help us have Christmas, does he? In these cases, put your answer in its larger context and explain that your partner doesn't believe as you do, but has other beliefs that are also worthy. Explain what you as parents decided to do about his religious upbringing. Throughout, make it apparent that both faiths have a great deal to offer and although they are different, they are both good. This will be a lesson in tolerance as well as giving him the sense that no doors are closed until he closes them.

The first inkling you may have that he is beginning to see himself in one faith or the other is when he begins to complain, "How come I'm the only Jewish kid who has to go to Easter services," or "Why am I the only kid in my class who has to learn these *zemirot* (Jewish 'table hymns' sung at the opening of Sabbath)?!" These kinds of declarations may simply be to get out of doing something he doesn't want to do just then. Or they may be driven by his desire to be with his friends. They also may be indicative, however, of his religious interests. If they are persistent, you might talk with him about why he feels this way. Changing back and forth from one religion to another is not helpful, especially when it is done on a whim. Some parents will agree to let him make a decision about which religion he would like to choose at some significant point in the not-too-distant future, say, when he moves into junior high, or has his tenth birthday. Over the ensuing months, possibly years, you all will be able to see if he has indeed settled on a particular choice.

In middle school and junior high, your child may begin to express more thoughtful preferences. If you have cultivated ongoing conversations over time you will have helped him to be able to clarify his ideas and his sense of religious identity and make decisions about his future religious directions. You might ask him some questions to encourage him to consider his religious tradition more deeply, especially as his peer group is likely to be planning to join their religious communities as full members. Again, his response should be a genuine choice that is acted upon. Work with him to carry through his decision.

Be prepared for the fact that no matter what your combined endeavors have been directed toward, there is always the possibility that your child will eventually decide differently. With the opportunity to practice making choices and talking through his reasons throughout all his growing years, he will be as well prepared to make a lifelong choice of religious faith as you are able to make for him.

In middle teen years, a young person has the skills and knowledge necessary to examine the history of his parents' faiths and to begin to explore their meaningfulness and relevance to his own life. During these years and later, he is likely to be characterized by an idealism and a desire to belong that can either attract him more profoundly or repel him from a faith tradition. By his mid to late teens, you may have little influence over your child's religious direction other than to encourage him in developing his own chosen commitments.

27

FINDING COMMON GROUND

The focus until now has been on the differences a couple might face when they come from different religious backgrounds and how they might deal with these differences in the raising of their child. It is in the divide between faiths that tensions, conflicts, and opposing dynamics occur. It is here that parents need to be open, honest, decisive, and creative in seeking to find the solutions they believe will work best in their family. At this point, an otherwise potentially happy marriage can founder.

What the discussion so far has not touched on is the common ground that exists between faiths, even faiths that seem disparate. Some of the deep divergences between religions are a matter of history. Long ago, two faiths may have separated, not necessarily in goodwill, and the antagonisms have persisted long after the causes have ceased to be relevant. Many people today feel that this describes the relationship among the various Protestant Christian groups and between Protestants and Catholics. Other differences are as much an outworking of cultural preferences and how particular communities express their faith as substantive differences in the faith itself. Muslims in Saudi Arabia, Pakistan, and Bosnia, and Black Muslims in North America, for instance, actually share more common ground than cursory appearances would suggest.

In an interfaith family, parents and their children have a unique opportunity to explore the common ground that their faiths occupy. These shared elements may be woven into their solution and certainly used to connect their children to both faiths. Such a process of discovery helps overcome some of the disruptive and artificial barriers that may have been built over centuries. It will certainly prepare your child to accept differences more comfortably and to rise above some of the petty parochialism that has divided people from each other.

The following are areas of commonality you might explore.

- *A shared God to worship*
  Three major world religions worship the same God: Judaism, Christianity, and Islam. They may have different names for God and they do have different worship practices, but Hashem of Jewish belief, God of Christian belief, and Allah of the Muslim faith is essentially the same deity. Here, then, some significant connections might be made between an interfaith couple, and with their children. They might compare common beliefs such as:
  — there is only one God;
  — God was there in the beginning of time and will be there until the end of time;
  — God is just, merciful, and loving;
  — God knows best how people should live;
  — God requires obedience;
  — God is our judge;
  — God cares for us;
  — We cannot know God fully, but we can learn about God;
  — When we glimpse God in faith we are drawn to worship.
- *Shared history*
  Faiths have grown up within particular cultures, but throughout history there have been numerous occasions

123

when cultures have met. Even further back, many religions shared a common beginning. Again using the three monotheistic religions as an example, Jews, Christians, and Muslims incorporate into their own sense of origins the stories of the same early ancestors. So Christians accept all of the Jewish Scripture, to which they have added what they call the New Testament. Muslims accept the Jewish and Christian Scriptures, to which they have added the Qur'an. Abraham and Sarah are considered the parents of the Jewish and Islamic nations. The most sacred place of worship for Muslims is Mecca, thought to be the burial place of Abraham. All three faiths share the stories of Adam and Eve, of Moses, Daniel, and Jonah. Muslims speak reverently of Jesus. Such interactions are also possible between other faiths as well. Hinduism finds some roots in Buddhism, and Taoism in Confucianism, for instance. Interfaith families can introduce their children to these shared histories.

- *Shared teachings*
Although each faith is distinct, many teachings are shared by all faiths. This is especially true of teachings about how people should live. Every faith tradition has its version of the Golden Rule. All religions teach believers how to treat others, including strangers, with kindness and justice, to do good to those who are in need, such as the poor and outcast, to be honest in business dealings, to respect parents and elders, to take care in raising the young, and so on. Parents will find they have much in common when it comes to their child's character formation.

- *Shared sense of the sacred*
All faiths look for meaning beyond mere survival in the material world. For some, this lies in God, for others in some other construct of infinity or the supernatural. To communicate this "something beyond" religions have set aside special places—churches, mosques, temples, shrines, and other sa-

cred places—where people can worship. They have designated special times—Sabbaths, annual festivals, prayer times—so people can devote their attention to spiritual activities. They have developed special ways for people to communicate with the sacred—prayers, singing, meditation, and rituals. When you look beyond the immediate differences between faiths, you see that they all have a sense of the sacred and attempt to be in touch with the holy by some means. There is a common reaching toward that which touches the human spirit most profoundly.

In overcoming the distraction of differences between faiths, you are better able to learn from each other. In this recognition you can begin to shore up your own beliefs by giving them new dimensions and new insights gained from another's faith. Once parents have come to appreciate their partner's sense of the sacred, they will have a rich heritage to share with their children.

28

WHEN FAITHS CANNOT MIX

The common ground on which all faiths stand has produced a variety of religions, just like a garden into which a handful of mixed flower seeds has been scattered produces an array of different plants. These flowers all have their own kinds of leaves and produce different blooms and perfumes. Their life cycles vary and the seeds that form as the flowers die off take on different characteristics. Not all flowers are compatible with each other: plants sometimes require different conditions and they may struggle against one another for survival. In the world of religions, differences appear as alternate pictures of God, as opposing doctrines, as diverging expressions of worship, as different scriptures, and, one could say, as different cultures. Just as no two species of plants are identical, so no two religions are exactly the same.

Sometimes the differences between faiths are so antagonistic they cannot mix well together. Imagine this scenario. John and Jane are of different faiths. Let's say Jane is Jewish, and knows that her children will be considered Jewish if she brings them up in her faith. Let's further allow that she is proud of her heritage, believing it to be a rich and worthwhile tradition in which to raise children. Say, too, that she also suspects that Christianity is nothing more than a mistaken offshoot from Judaism that developed a whole mythology around a Jewish man, Jesus, who was very charismatic and won a great following, but who was only a mere man in the final analysis. More than that, she argues that Jews have suffered terribly at the hands of Christians for two thousand years, the most recent and horrible instance being the Holocaust.

Now let's imagine John as a self-proclaimed born-again Christian. He earnestly believes that the Jews rejected Jesus as the Messiah, and in fact, conspired to have him crucified, so God rejected them and instead called Christians to be the chosen people to represent God on earth. Consequently, he is sure that he is called by God to witness about his Christian faith and attempts to persuade others, including Jane, to convert and join his church. Assume that he is prompted to undertake this task by the firm conviction that those who do not believe in Jesus as the Savior will be eternally lost.

Now, imagine further that John and Jane are otherwise attracted to each other. Friends predict that marriage might even be down the road for them. Clearly, their religious differences do not mix well. What are their choices for creating a peaceful and harmonious relationship? While there is no easy solution, here are some alternatives they might consider:

- *Ignore the problems.*
  John and Jane could go about their courtship sidestepping all the time the thing that most divides them—their religious beliefs and practices. Knowing that this is a touchy subject, they could put their efforts into always pleasing their partner. This is not easy, but easier before they set up home together than after. And herein lies the fatal flaw in this strategy. Ignoring their religious differences does not solve them; it only postpones them. Sooner or later, the matter is going to have to be addressed and this task becomes progressively more difficult as expectations solidify and other accompanying decisions are made, such as where they will spend

Christmas, and when they will see each other, and where they will be married. Ignoring problems is only a temporary solution and not a satisfying one at that.

- *Agree to disagree.*

Clearly, if John and Jane are going to see their relationship grow, at the very least they are going to have to admit that they do not see eye-to-eye on the matter of religion. They will have to live with the knowledge that they each believe the other to be wrong, and, conversely, are believed to be wrong by the other. Jane should acknowledge that she will always think John has taken on a poorer belief system and tradition than her own. John will have to find a way of accepting his conviction that his partner is going to be eternally lost. For both of them, this is not going to be easy, but unless they can at least agree to disagree they could very well end up with a lifetime of argument and conflict. Unfortunately, this resolution to their differences does little in helping them to decide what to do about their child's religious development.

- *Let each other be.*

There is a fine line between disagreeing with what your partner is doing and allowing him to do it nevertheless. This goes a step beyond agreeing to disagree, which merely admits that there are differences. Here, each one gives to the other the full freedom without resistance to act out those differences. Jane would attend synagogue, maintain a kosher kitchen for herself if she chose to, and celebrate the seasons of the Jewish religious year. John would not constantly cite scripture to her, try to get her to read his church pamphlets, and invite her to come to evangelistic meetings at his church. He would, however, be free to participate fully in the activities of his church, including standing on street corners witnessing to strangers about his faith. Jane would not complain if he went to meetings not only all day Sunday but Wednesday evening as well. This letting the other be what they want to be does resolve some of the tension of constant harassment and trying to change the other's mind. What it still leaves unresolved, however, is what should be done about their child's religious upbringing.

• *Compromise.*

One can imagine that compromise is not a welcome notion for either Jane or John, since both prefer to hold steadfast to their own faith tradition. However, it is a way to find a meeting ground between their differences that will make for a more harmonious home for the sake of any children they might have. In this regard, it carries them a step further than letting the other be, for it suggests that they will actively cooperate to establish this common ground between them. Jane may agree, for instance, to give up her dreams of having a kosher kitchen so John can have his familiar foods. John may agree to limit his attendance at services so they might spend more time together. They may both find their way toward being less critical of the other's faith, especially as they come to appreciate something of the value their partner finds in it. They may occasionally accompany each other to services and welcome each other's religious friends at social gatherings. Although Hanukkah is relatively insignificant to Jane, she will celebrate it along with John's Christmas holiday each year so they can enjoy the season together. While this solution does not determine how their child shall be raised, it does provide a more congenial environment for making that decision and for carrying it out. It does, however, mean that both have given up something in the hopes of gaining something they both want, a happy home together.

• *Convert.*

Either Jane or John could decide to give up their faith and join their partner's community. For Jane this would mean putting aside her prejudices against Jesus and being baptized a Christian. It would mean attending services on Sunday instead of Saturday. She would not be permitting her children to accept fully the Jewish heritage she could pass on to them. For John, on the other hand, it would mean renouncing the New Testament and accepting the Old Testament as the complete scripture. It could mean undergoing the ritual of circumcision. He would be wise to learn a whole new liturgy, along with some Hebrew, so that his participation would be more meaningful.

A study released by the American Jewish Committee in 1983 under the direction of Egon Mayer suggests that a child brought up Jewish in an interfaith home where one parent converted to Judaism is likely to be more "Jewish" than other Jewish children. This finding probably holds true across other faiths as well, because few things are more absorbing and transforming than a new-found faith. Borrowing a phrase from John the Revelator, Christians sometimes call this experience "first love," comparing it with those heady and totally exciting days of first falling in love. When a partner willingly and wholeheartedly converts to the faith of her spouse, not only does she bring to her parenting all the freshness and wonder of her new religious experience but she might also stimulate a new vigor in her spouse's faith as well. In *Mixed Blessings,* Rachel and Paul Cowan tell the story of Rachel's conversion and what it meant to them both. It is a personal account well worth reading for its description of both the joys and fears of such a choice. Together, such a couple can become a powerful team working for the religious education of their child. Conversion clearly solves the problem of how the children will be raised, but one partner in particular does have to make profound life changes.

• *Separate.*
This may be the most difficult choice of all—at least in the

short term. If John and Jane find that their faiths really do not mix, and from all appearances this could very well be true, and if none of the other solutions appeals to them, then the best thing they can do for their own and each other's happiness is to go their separate ways. Better to suffer the loss of a potential partner than to have to deal with a lifetime of conflict and strife in the home over religion. Better yet if they can spare any future children they might have from being caught in the middle of their religious differences. By the accounts of grown children from such families, such an environment can pass on a legacy of bitterness, anger, and alienation to their children. If a child comes into the family before John and Jane have resolved their religious tensions, then conflicts between them will only be magnified. Having a child brings enormous changes to how parents think and feel. They naturally want the very best for her, and this desire becomes inevitably entangled with the value they find in their faith.

Each of these suggestions has its own set of difficulties. Every step toward solving some problem creates a new set of hazards to be dealt with. In other words, there is no comprehensive solution to finding a way of mixing strongly divergent faiths. You will notice that each successive solution is more demanding than the previous one—but possibly more effective in the long run. It is possible that the more effort undertaken and the greater the sacrifices made at the outset, the more lasting and peaceful the resolution to very pronounced differences in religious faith may be.

Part Four

~~~~~~

MEETING CHALLENGES

When a couple has made a choice about the religious faith or faiths they will raise their child in, they will then want to think more specifically about how they will transform their decision into practice. Planning in the abstract is one matter; making the plan a reality can be a different matter altogether. In an interfaith family, teaching religious beliefs and enacting religious observances at home requires special thought. Who will teach what? How will she or he teach it? What rituals are appropriate for this family? Who will be included in the ritual? Another set of decisions revolves around making plans for religious instruction outside of the immediate family circle. What services will your child attend and how will she be prepared for them? What school will he attend and what factors should be considered in making such a choice? Then there are the challenges of dealing with pressures that might come from family and friends. How does the family plan to meet these? And because faith is dynamic, parents as well as children grow and change in faith. As you nurture your own commitments and beliefs, how will the family respond to the transitions you might pass through? And finally, how can your interfaith family maximize the benefits to your child of growing up with differences? As each question is addressed, an array of practical solutions and strategies will be offered for you to consider.

29

~~~~~~

TEACHING RELIGIOUS BELIEFS AT HOME

Growing up in a religious faith almost always involves learning the ways of that religion. This continues throughout the child's growing years and many religious groups prepare teaching materials and learning activities to assist parents in this instruction. The process takes on special importance as the child reaches his teen years because most faiths provide some kind of initiation service for entry into full membership. For Jews, there is the bar mitzvah; Christians have confirmation or baptism services; and some Hindus have the thread ceremony for the young men. In every case, the young person must demonstrate his knowledge of the beliefs and practices of the faith so that he may begin participating along with adult members.

Religious organizations realize that instructing the young is something that they cannot undertake alone, but that is more effective when it is reinforced in the home. This can pose a set of problems for the interfaith family. What role does each parent play in this instruction? When should this instruction take place? How can both parents make the exercise as profitable and enjoyable for the child as possible?

As a parent, you are a religious educator—whether you know it or not. By your actions, attitudes, and spoken word, you will be teaching your child what to believe, how to act, and what to value. It is better to acknowledge this basic verity and plan for it than to presume that your part in the process does not matter. Although both parents have a role to play, the responsibilities and challenges will be different depending on whether the child is to be brought up in your faith or your partner's.

- *If the child is to be raised in your faith . . .*

  . . . you obviously bear the major responsibility for his religious instruction in the home. You have the better knowledge and experience of the faith, you understand the inner workings of the religion, and you probably have more contact with those who can help with this instruction. You are fortunate to be able to pass on your faith heritage to your child.

  Set aside a regular time and place for religious instruction and make this as least disruptive to the family schedule as possible. Some parents like to read scripture stories to their children as bedtime stories, others prefer to do this first thing in the morning or after supper, while still others limit their efforts to the weekend. You may choose to sit together around the dinner table or go to the den or family room or the place where the child does his homework. When the time and the place is predictable, your partner can work with you more easily to maintain the quiet attention you want to give to the instruction.

  Plan how you can use the time effectively. Published activities are often available through your local congregation. Not all instruction has to consist of you giving your child information. You might undertake a project together, such as memorizing chosen scriptures, reading daily devotionals together, studying Hebrew, building a model of the ark, making a poster of Creation Week, or creating depictions of the Stations of the Cross.

Avoid criticizing your partner's beliefs. Even when the child passes judgment on or asks you a direct question about these beliefs, you do not have to be drawn into saying something derogatory. Rather, explain that these ideas are simply different from your own, adding that you both love this parent nevertheless.

• *If your child is being raised in your partner's faith* . . .

. . . you have a unique set of responsibilities and challenges as a supporter of his religious instruction. This role can be as demanding as your partner's more direct involvement. Above all, avoid working at cross purposes with your partner or undermining in any one of a thousand subtle ways the efforts being undertaken to give your child a grounding in a faith tradition.

Imagine you and your family at the 4th of July fireworks display. Your partner has been working with your child in daily Bible studies for preschoolers and some of the ideas are beginning to take hold. As you watch the skyrockets lift toward the clouds, your son watches in wonder and asks you, in all seriousness, whether they can reach God. But you do not accept the traditional formulations of God. Remembering that a great deal of religious instruction happens casually in just these kinds of situations, how shall you answer? The younger the child, the more important it is to avoid confusing him with alternative viewpoints. You might say, "Oh no. God is way higher than the clouds, the moon, and the stars." If you do not want to answer so affirmatively, you might respond with a question of your own that will help him clarify his own ideas. "What do you think?" "What have you learned about where God lives?" "Where is heaven?" "Do you think the skyrockets can reach as high as a big tree? a mountain?

an airplane? God?" As a last resort, you might suggest he ask
your partner the same question. In any event, find a way of
answering that supports your partner's efforts.

There is always the temptation to use religion as some
kind of weapon against your partner or child when things are
not going well. If you want to alienate your family, you might
respond to your child's misbehavior with words such as: "So,
that's what they teach you at Sunday School!"

Your level of involvement should be determined by your
level of comfort. At the lowest level, the non-believing parent
avoids negative comments, conflicting schedules, and under-
handed contradictions. Simply failing to do no wrong is usually not as satisfying as doing good. Many parents would
prefer to be more pro-active. With very young children, for
instance, you may be willing to tell a Bible story. You may
support your partner by insisting that the child give the required time and attention to the instruction. As he grows,
you may hear memory verses, teach Hebrew vocabulary, help
him plan and carry out a religious education project, or supervise his study time. The older child may be supported by
your endorsement and encouragement as he plans for his
initiation into full membership. Show him in real ways that
you approve of his progress and are proud of his growing
religious knowledge. Throughout all his years, you can be the
kind of listener and questioner who prompts your child to
think carefully about his religious ideas as they form in his
heart and mind.

30

~~~~~~

ENACTING RELIGIOUS OBSERVANCES IN THE HOME

Whereas religious instruction can be done privately in the home, enacting religious observances is usually a more public undertaking. That is, your child may work more or less alone in her bedroom on her daily religious lesson, but many observances take place throughout the home. For instance, besides the prayer before bedtime, there may be prayers before meals, prayers on a prayer mat five times a day, prayers to greet the Sabbath, and so on. While memorizing scripture might take place at the kitchen table after dinner and not intrude on what the rest of the family is doing, Christmas decorations, menorahs, and shrines are meant to be obvious. Fasting times observed by many faiths, prohibitions against particular foods such as pork for Jews and Muslims, regulations about how foods are to be prepared such as kosher meats, celebratory foods such as Easter eggs and matzoh balls, and ritualized meals such as Christmas dinner or the Seder on the eve of the Jewish Passover are intrusive on the whole family. Dealing with religious observances in the home builds on the principles already suggested for religious instruction in the home, but since religious observances bring their own special challenges to both the believing and non-believing parent, here are some further considerations.

- *If the child is being raised in your faith . . .*

  . . . you walk the fine line between full expression of that faith with your child and the restraint on that expression in respect of your partner's faith. Simply put, if you are Jewish and your partner is Christian, for instance, your home cannot be 100% Jewish—that would be a denial and marginalization of your partner's faith. With this in mind, you need to determine together how the time and space for religious observances will be shared. Even though the child is to be exposed primarily to your faith, your partner should still be free to meet his religious obligations.

  This is where negotiation is crucial. If you have a Christmas tree for your child, can you also light Hanukkah candles? If you say grace before each meal, can your partner also unroll his prayer mat to pray? During Easter, can the whole family participate in the Passover Seder? If you are going to fast before Mass, can you cooperate with your partner as he observes Ramadan by fasting and postponing sexual relations? One of the foundations for this negotiation is the recognition that you both pray, you both eat special foods, you both fast, you both decorate your home, you both recognize holy times, and you both commemorate significant events in the past—you simply do these things in different ways. Your negotiations then are primarily over how you can accommodate these differences in expression.

  Negotiation usually means that both parties do not get all that they would normally expect. Although you may come out with more of what you would wish because your faith is being shared with your child, you should still ensure that your partner's needs are being met. There will be less of a negative impact on the growing faith of the child and more chance of enrichment by witnessing other expressions of faith.

• *If the child is being raised in your partner's faith . . .*

. . . then your space and time will sometimes be involved. How you choose to respond to this is a function of your goodwill and level of comfort. You may begrudgingly watch it all happen and complain if either your child or your partner nudges the boundaries you have drawn in your mind. You could noisily begin your meal while grace is being offered, if you wanted to. You could turn the TV up loudly during prayers, if you chose. You could accidentally knock a candlestick over, if you were not careful. But how would that help your relationship with your partner or your child? How would that promote your own faith?

Of course, you don't have to act negatively toward the faith of others to protect your own. Nor do you effectively cultivate a respect for differences by these kinds of actions. What you might accomplish is an alienation and resentment between you and the rest of the family. It is better for the whole family's peace of mind, faith development, and religious self-expression if you choose rather to celebrate consistently your own religious observances while helping the rest of the family celebrate theirs. Modeling this kind of pluralism in the home makes for a spiritual environment in which you all can flourish.

31

ATTENDING SERVICES

Naturally, belonging to a faith tradition involves community meetings. These usually occur on a regular basis: in the case of Muslim prayers, daily at the mosque; in the case of Hindu worship, several times a week for many worshipers at a temple; in the case of Jewish and Christian congregations, at least weekly at synagogue or church; and in the case of many faiths, special high holy occasions according to a yearly calendar. Community gatherings might also involve pilgrimages to sacred places or large combined meetings where not only worship but also the business of the community is conducted. Some religious groups have intermittent periods of intense religious worship, such as revivals or retreats.

Into this picture must be added the social dimensions of belonging to a religious community. Many congregations have activity clubs for different age groups so that they might enjoy the company of people of the same faith in recreation, learning a skill, pursuing a mutual hobby, or acting as a support group for each other. It is not uncommon to find a new parents' league, a teenage club, or a grief support group. The friends a family will make at religious gatherings may sometimes visit each other. Volunteer service is often undertaken in religious circles, so groups of members will operate a soup kitchen, set up a boys or girls club in the inner city, or fly to some distant place to build a school or meeting place for a disadvantaged congregation. So in a number of ways, formal and informal groups of believers will meet and work together.

This can pose a special challenge to the interfaith family. Some members of the family will worship and move in social circles of which their partners are not a part. For them, friendships will develop and interests will be pursued with others that at some level exclude their spouses. Watching your partner and children leave for weekly services can be a very lonely experience. It is lonely not only for the partner who remains at home; it is also lonely for the partner who goes into the congregational setting alone. How can this alienation be minimized?

• *If your child is being raised in your faith . . .*
. . . widen your social circle. It is very tempting to worship and socialize with people of your own faith because you talk the same talk, share the same history, hold the same values, eat the same foods, celebrate the same seasons, and mark each other's births, comings of age, marriages, and deaths together. A congregation can provide a consistency to your child's environment, ensuring that values, beliefs, and practices carry across to work, play, and worship. Parents in a community of believers share many of the same hopes and fears for their children. However, as an interfaith couple, you have other sources of social support to call upon—at least, those of your partner.

You cannot determine your child's best friend, but you can expose him to numerous playmates. You cannot make your daughter enjoy a particular children's club, but you can give her the opportunity to choose from a number of good alternatives, both within and outside your congregation. You cannot always refuse to eat with your church friends, but you can invite your partner to join you. You should not always expect to socialize only with people from your religious community and never with your partner's friends. Your home can be open to many people, many interests, and many opportunities to serve others and include the pursuits and concerns of your partner, your child, and yourself.

- *If your child is being raised in your partner's faith . . .*
. . . do not remain a stranger to the people in his community. You can get to know them in a number of ways. Don't absent yourself on the grounds that they share something you do not want. Join them on the grounds that you can share something with them that you all might want—good friendship, companions in undertaking a service project, a safe and nurturing environment for your child to grow in, and so on. Welcome them into your home. Plan family outings that can include them. Make provision for the exercise of their faith while they are with you so they will feel comfortable. Find occasions, maybe weddings and funerals, and possibly some special events like Mother's or Father's Day celebrations for starters, when you can sometimes attend services with the rest of the family.

An interfaith couple can overcome the potential alienation they might otherwise experience as one makes connections with a community of believers that the other does not, when both of them reach out inclusively to the other. Do not limit yourself to the immediate faith community you know, but develop a wide circle of relationships and friendships that your child can experience with you. Do not keep away from your partner's faith community, but reach out in friendship if not in mutual belief to them, so that you can share as fully as you are able your child's faith community.

32

CHOOSING A SCHOOL

C hoosing the school your child will attend can be a particularly contentious issue between parents of different faiths. Even when the agreement is to raise the child in one faith, the parents may disagree over this point. The partner who is sharing his faith with the child may expect that doing this wholeheartedly entails sending her to a religious school. The other partner may want to draw the line a little sooner than that, arguing that attendance at services, religious instruction at home and church, synagogue, or mosque, and the number of prayers and other rituals permitted in the home is enough. And both have a case.

- *The case for religious school.*
  At a religious school, the lessons taught at home and the place of worship are extended. With trained teachers and many resources for learning, the instruction is likely to be more systematic, matching the child's developmental level more closely, and dealt with at a deeper level. Most parochial schools will have religious instruction daily, curricula are developed for that purpose, and the school schedule accommodates religious observances. The child is not subject to the same hazards that accompany being different when the whole school subscribes ostensibly to the same practices.

    Furthermore, the school can teach aspects of the faith that the home and worship place is usually not so well prepared to teach. In some religions, there is a language to learn, such as Hebrew, Arabic, or Sanskrit. Sometimes there are children's choirs that require a great deal of rehearsal time. For example, the Anglican tradition has some very fine choir schools that combine liturgical and music studies with the normal curriculum. Even apart from these specialized aspects of religious study, the learning conducted by trained teachers and scholars is likely to be more rigorous and, for older students, more critical so that counter-arguments can be studied to broaden the student's appreciation and defense of the faith.

Another major advantage of parochial education is that the student body, the faculty, and the curriculum are closer in line with the ideals of the religious community than another school would be. So there is a consistency in the environment in which the child is growing. The teachers, on the whole, accept the same tenets of faith, the students have similar understandings, and all the subjects of the curriculum are brought into harmony with religious belief. The child is, therefore, spared the confusion of competing ideas and contradictions.

Further, she has teachers who are interested in her spiritual development and may nurture her faith in appropriate ways. The faculty in religious schools often accept lower salaries, but their commitment to their faith draws them to make this sacrifice. Their students see not only their teaching but also their commitment, and so these adults become both mentors and models.

- *The case against religious school.*
The interfaith couple, however, may not see all these factors as advantages. They may regard the religious focus as too narrow. All the child's learning may point in the same direction and be grounded on the same foundation of beliefs, but she is deprived of the opportunity to confront other tradi-

tions and ideas and people significantly different from herself. She may never have to defend her faith or test the depth of her loyalty to it in an environment that is totally supportive of it.

She will learn throughout her schooling to trust those who teach her and accept what they have told her. This could mean she is more vulnerable to persuasion from others who might have a different set of basic beliefs. If she were to go to another school, she would become used to hearing different ideas and learn along the way to be more critical about what she accepts as true and valuable.

Mixing primarily with people of the same faith can create a ghettoized mentality. Your child may become isolated from the rest of the world, suspicious and judgmental of others. A kind of aloofness and sense of superiority may set in for some. Others may grow up feeling different and maybe even a little deprived of some of the experiences of others and take on a sense of embarrassed inferiority. At the least, they may not be comfortable in social situations different from the easy relationships they have formed among people of their faith.

This narrowness can be a problem in any family, but it may be felt most keenly in an interfaith home. The parent of a different faith may become increasingly isolated from the rest of the family, being the only one who comfortably moves in different social circles. The "otherness" that he represents is limited in serving as a bridge between the home and the pluralistic world beyond.

Like all child-rearing decisions, the choice of schooling is one that requires negotiation and forethought. In considering the case for and against religious schooling for your child, look for ways you can compensate for the weaknesses of the choice you make while maximizing its strengths. For instance, you may choose to enroll your child at the church school but also insist on her joining the local basketball team to meet girls of other religious persuasions. Other factors will have to weigh into your choice as well: the relative quality of the religious school compared with other schools in the neighborhood, your child's preferences, affordability (religious school fees can be quite steep), and the school's location. At least, in approaching this decision, be aware of the array of factors that prevail and plan together on how you will deal with them.

33

~~~~~~

RESOLVING CONFLICT ALONG THE WAY

S ome highly charged moments in the life of a family can be especially disruptive of the plans you have made for dealing with your religious differences. In *If I'm Jewish and You're Christian, What Are the Kids?* Andrea King illustrates with case studies some of these crisis points: divorce and remarriage, the birth of a child, the death of a parent, or the death of a child. These events, which are traumatic for any family, can take on added painfulness as the family wrestles with the religious issues that might be involved. The matter of custody, mourning rituals, family heritage, and expectations can all be colored by religious preferences that none of you might have predicted beforehand.

No matter how well prepared a couple might think they are for dealing with their interfaith differences, even in the absence of a major family crisis, some disagreements and misunderstandings along the way are inevitable. You might chalk this up to human nature, but may still be left wondering why human nature turns out this way. Sometimes you can be more precise about the causes.

Remember Janet and Mark in Key 8? Janet is a fundamentalist Christian while Mark's beliefs and commitments are more liberal. With a little prompting from Janet's dad, the couple began some serious planning about their lives together, especially about how they would raise their child. They felt they were just about as ready as they could be to face any decision points along the way. As it turned out, however, they still had some conflicts to deal with.

They discovered, for instance, that while they both agreed wholeheartedly that Janet would take the children with her to church and teach them her faith at home, when their son Jonathan was born, this decision took on new dimensions. Janet was more excited than ever as she looked forward to having the baby dedicated at the church service and enrolled in the infants' Sunday School class. As Mark looked at this new little baby, however, he began to have second thoughts about this plan. He wanted to introduce him to his congregation. He imagined him in the starring role at the upcoming Christmas pageant. He thought he would like to see him with the other children in choir robes singing at the weekly service. Actually having a baby helped to sharpen their respective dreams for their child. Somehow in their earlier planning, Mark always imagined they would have a girl. It seemed right for this imaginary child to be with her mother. But Jonathan was a son, and that put a new twist on things.

When Janet and Mark laid their plans, they were rather starry-eyed, as they recognize now looking back. Janet could do no wrong in Mark's eyes and vice versa. They wanted to please each other, no matter what. The three years they have been married have brought some changes. In some ways their affection for each other is deeper and more meaningful, but they have also come to realize their partner is not perfect in every way, nor are they as willing to give in to each other as they once were. To complicate matters, there were some issues they thought they could take care of when the time came.

Schooling was one decision they didn't make and now it looms ahead of them.

This couple is not unique by any means. The change in focus a baby can bring, the maturing of the couple's relationship, and the many large and small decisions that have to be made can be sources of contention. Conflict, however, is an opportunity for creative problem-solving. Here are some suggestions for dealing with tensions in a productive way.

- *Choose the time carefully.*
  One thing Mark and Janet should avoid is discussing their differences when they are tired after a day's work, when the baby is crying, or when in-laws are about to arrive. They have some fairly significant matters to sort out, so they should begin their discussion in a good frame of mind. They may need to plan the right moment—say after lunch on Saturday afternoon when Jonathan is likely to be asleep and the morning's chores are already behind them. Incidentally, having had a few days to think about things, they will likely be more articulate about their desires and maybe even a little more conciliatory toward each other.
- *Lay out your wishes and reasons.*
  If Mark wants to send Jonathan to public school and Janet wants to send him to church school, they need to be able to tell each other quite honestly what they want and why they believe their plan is better. This gives them both something to grapple with that goes beyond just their respective emotional responses. This may require a little combined homework on their parts, checking out the two schools, talking with the teachers, examining their budget, and so on.

  In such a process, however, they should not overlook the power of feelings. In *The Intermarriage Handbook*, Judy Petsonk and Jim Remsen go so far as to claim that the intimacy of sharing your feelings with each other is the very foundation for the solutions you will eventually find. They suggest this intimacy can be established if you follow a few simple rules: Be honest about how you feel; be careful not to blame your partner for how you feel (that is, don't say, "You make me angry when you . . . ," but rather, "I am angry when you . . . "); agree that only one of you will speak at a time; don't take your partner's strong feelings personally; and restate your partner's point so that she knows you understand what she is saying. Until you have shared your feelings about the issue, you will not be able to resolve it.

- *Avoid making accusations.*

Mark might be tempted to accuse Janet of trying to please her parents because he knows they, too, would like to see Jonathan in the church school—Janet's dad is the school board chairman, after all. On the other hand, Janet might be tempted to accuse Mark of being unfair because he had agreed a long time ago to bring up their child in her faith. But where would these accusations get them? Probably farther apart than ever. If they really do carry these suspicions, they can introduce them into the conversation with a much more helpful tone.

Mark might say, "Honey, I'm really afraid that your parents might be putting too much pressure on us about this. What do you think?"

Janet might say, "I thought you were happy with our decision to raise Jonathan in my church. How can we do this best if we do not send him to church school?"

- *Search for middle ground.*

If Janet and Mark fail to convince each other and remain just as sure of their position as before, they may need to work deliberately on finding middle ground. By nature, this middle ground is created by compromise. In its basic form, each gives something in order to get something. They could agree to send Jonathan to church school for his elementary education and to the public middle school when the time came. Or, they may prefer to send him to public school for all his schooling but permit him to join in all the activities at his mother's church on weekends to maintain continuity with his friends there. To find this middle ground they both need to contribute their best creative energies.

Conflict may not be avoidable, but neither need it be insurmountable. Every couple faces points in their relationship that have to be thoughtfully negotiated and creatively resolved. Religious disagreements are often more emotionally charged than others, but can be dealt with in the same way. Fortunately, the skills of negotiation and creative problem-solving improve with practice, and so are best called upon sooner rather than later.

34

~~~~~~

DEALING WITH PRESSURE FROM FAMILY AND FRIENDS

Setting up house with someone of a different faith can be a big step to take not only for you but for your family and circle of friends. Jeannette was raised a Christian but during her teenage and early adult life she had been in and out of trouble with the police over drugs and related problems. Her family were beside themselves. She was unhappy within herself, couldn't settle down in a job, and didn't know what to do with her life—that is, until she met a Muslim family in her apartment building. They got to talking. She got to listening for the first time in a long time. She visited the mosque and began to study Islam. Her conversion brought profound changes to her life. Where she had drifted before, now her days were structured around prayers, fasting, and visits to the mosque. Her clothing changed as she took to wearing the veils of Muslim women. Through her new community she met a Muslim man. They planned to live in Iran after they were married. All along, these tremendous changes in her life were reverberating through her entire family. As they had not been watching her earlier deterioration with indifference, neither were they looking on passively to the current transformations she was now undergoing. Despite the obvious improvement in her outlook and behavior, religion was one change they would not have anticipated or chosen.

Of all the people in your circle of relationships that have the biggest adjustments to make to your interfaith home, your parents are likely to be the most affected. Even if you have prepared them as well as possible, your parents may not be able to adjust to your decision. Just as you have dreams and plans for your child, so they had them for you. And they had these dreams not only for you but for their grandchildren, too. If they have always belonged to a religious community and raised you in that faith, they are probably going to want to see your child in that faith as well. If you and your partner have decided differently, there will be some tensions to deal with.

Families may express disappointment—often, you may see pained expressions on their faces. It may feel as if they are nagging you. They may use baby-sitting occasions to get their message across to your child. Children being raised in the Christian faith have received prayer shawls as birthday presents and Jewish children have been given Bibles at Christmas time. One couple, whose child was being raised Jewish, discovered that grandma threatened to have the child secretly baptized. This particular dilemma was further compounded by the fact that if the parents were to enroll the child in Hebrew school, he would have to undergo a formal conversion ceremony because the synagogue would refuse to accept a "baptized" child into its program. Children have been abducted by families or held by separated parents to give them a particular religious upbringing, as Betty Mahmoody's story, *Not Without My Daughter*, reveals. Interfaith couples often declare that they could manage the multidimensional aspects of raising their child in a home that celebrates two faiths if it weren't for the pressure and interference from family and friends.

In the worst cases, you and your partner may come to resent having to visit your folks and friends knowing you will be subjected to questions and criticisms about your child's upbringing. As Helene Arnstein observes in her study of relationships, *Between Mother-in-law and Daughter-in-law,* some families will never forgive you for not converting to their child's faith, and we might add, your own family may never forgive you if you do convert.

What can a couple do under these circumstances? You might try one or more of these alternative strategies:

- *Threaten.*
  This is often the easiest option and usually the most ineffective. Typical threats might be: "If you do not get off our backs about this, we will not come around anymore!" "If you cannot refrain from reading your religious stories to our girl when she stays over, we won't leave her here anymore!" If a threat is not carried out, it is useless. If it is carried out, everybody loses—you, your child, and your family and friends lose the pleasure of being with each other. Threats usually erupt when you have reached breaking point. Made under these conditions, they are usually given in anger and without much forethought. Better to consider your alternatives before you have reached this point.
- *Avoid.*
  Avoidance can take place at a number of levels. The most extreme is to avoid being with your family and friends. That might certainly take you out of reach of pressure from them at least for a time, but does not deal with the problem of the pressure itself. It is only effective when you are absent, and unless you want to be absent all the time, you will meet the pressure again on your next visit. Another level of avoidance is to dodge the subject when you are with family and friends. The difficulty with this strategy is that you end up feeling

like you live in a closet. You find you won't explain that you can't come to dinner because it is a fast day. You can't invite your family to your child's religious initiation. Your child cannot share with them some of the things she has been doing and enjoying. This kind of avoidance can raise suspicion and mistrust.

- *Confront.*

This is not easy by any means, but it may ameliorate the pressures you are under. Would a conversation like this help you? "Mom, Dad, we really want our children to know you and be with you. We want to come visit you. But we are not enjoying it as much as we wish we could. We know you are upset about our decision for Melissa's upbringing. We have explained to you why we chose that route. We need your cooperation. If you cannot give us that, can you at least give us the freedom to make our own decisions about her upbringing, as you made your decisions about how you raised your children? We are not going to change our minds about her religious training. If you cannot help us in this, then our visits will always be difficult and none of us want that to happen. So, how about it? Let's be friends and leave the subject alone." In confronting the family, find an ally—a grandparent, a sibling, an aunt or uncle, who can intervene for you or at least support you in the process.

- *Accept.*

Some couples realize that there is nothing they can do to change the opinions and behaviors of those they are close to. They acknowledge that they are not responsible for others' actions and have the equanimity to let them be. When there are hints and suggestions that they are not doing the right thing, they are able to smile and pass it off. When there are criticisms, they are able to say they are sorry their loved ones feel this way. When they see the subject coming up, they are able to change the topic of conversation. They seem to be

155

able to ride above being hurt or angry. This is easier to do if you as parents prepare and support each other for these visits.

It may be small consolation, but often the pressure that you experience from family and friends will gradually diminish as time goes by and you remain consistent and steadfast about your choices and decisions.

35

^^

MEETING CHANGES ALONG THE WAY

Interfaith partners who plan to set up house together are advised to talk about the future religious commitments of the home long before any child joins the family, and before they take the marriage vows. But even then, it is not uncommon for one partner or the other to have second thoughts farther down the road. The most difficult changes to deal with can be those involved in a complete change of mind by one member of the family.

In Key 28, you met a make-believe couple, John and Jane. He was imagined to be an enthusiastic, conservative Christian. Jane was pictured as a solid, convinced Jew. They seemed to have no easy solutions to their religious differences, especially when it came to choosing a faith for their child. Now imagine this same couple in all respects the same except for one detail. When they set up house together, John had no religious community at all. It was only after a few years, and with an addition or two to the family, that he converted and joined a conservative Christian community. The options for this imaginary situation are not the same as those for the earlier one, because agreements made between the couple when they got married have been in place for some time. Unfortunately, John now feels very strongly that he does not want his children to be brought up Jewish as they once agreed.

John and Jane's case is not unimaginable. As human beings go through life they experience a number of life-changing events that can transform their religious faith. In the opening to their book, *Mixed Blessings,* the Cowans tell their story of change and discovery. Rachel entered the marriage as a Unitarian with family roots that could be traced back to the *Mayflower;* Paul, as Jewish but non-observant. In fact, neither of them would have regarded themselves as particularly religious at all. Two decades later, Rachel converted and became a rabbinical student; Paul had been engaged in a personal quest to rediscover his Jewish roots. Their story illustrates the kind of events and personal encounters that can shape faith over time. One or another of a couple may convert. A traumatic experience can make one re-think one's priorities and commitments. The simple act of growing older and passing through crisis points in the maturing process can refocus faith. Some lose their former faith along the way. One may come to regret an earlier choice. The arrival of a baby and the probing questions children ask about faith can have a dramatic impact on the thinking of parents, especially about religious observances and beliefs.

The circumstances of a family may have changed so much that the former decisions no longer seem appropriate. The family may have moved, or the religious community may have changed in significant ways, or parents may have separated. Later in life, couples and their children may become an interfaith family.

Once decided, always decided, just doesn't work best for every family. And yet, the early agreement made in good faith between parents is usually not entered into lightly. It carries a sense of binding obligation. Most likely, both partners have invested a great deal of good will in it. Should parents revisit their former agreement? Is it wise or fair to make changes along the road? There is no simple answer to these questions, for the process can be very difficult for all concerned, not least for the child for whose sake the earlier agreement was made. How can a family survive these changes?

Getting back into balance requires many of the same kinds of negotiation strategies as those suggested for couples just starting out, except now the stakes may be higher.

- *If you are the one who has changed, then . . .*
  . . . taking the initiative for consensus building logically belongs to you. You are the one most likely to be dissatisfied with the current arrangements. You should raise the matter at a family council. Explain to your family what you are now thinking. Invite them to appreciate or at least understand these changes. With change often comes a new enthusiasm—you may want the world to change with you but, failing that, you may at least wish for some members of the family to join you. It is very easy to become insensitive and unreasonable at this time. Invite them to consider changes you may want them to make, but do not be coercive or attempt to intrude on their faith journey. Change cannot be forced. Although it may appear dramatic, change is something a person grows into until the moment is right. The strongest argument in favor of change is the quiet witness of a transformed life.
- *If your partner has changed, then . . .*
  . . . paradoxically he is the one least likely to be able to take the initiative in consensus building because he is caught up in the excitement of new ways of thinking. This does seem unfair, but being the one who least wants or needs change, you with your levelheadedness may have to take the lead. You may have to initiate reasoned discussion, for the sake of the whole family. Support your partner's faith development by making what adjustments you can. Find the opportunities

each new situation provides to enhance your child's sense of the sacred, always looking for bridges between you all. You may have to re-negotiate your agreements about your child's religious education, but always keep his religious development the central focus. You should be aware that in most cases, this means, "Do not disturb." In other words, unless you have good reason to believe otherwise, do not overturn your child's faith to substitute something new, because the danger is that he will lose faith altogether.

A thoroughgoing change in one family member can be disruptive, but it need not be destructive. Finding a way to accommodate it will require negotiation and maybe some compromise, but one person's change in faith does not give that individual the right to change the religious direction of everyone else in the family. What it does give your family is a new dimension in interfaith dialogue, providing an occasion for all to see religion in a larger light, while maintaining a faith of their own.

36

~~~~~~

PREPARING YOUR CHILD FOR A MULTIFAITH WORLD

Where once the United States was considered White, Anglo-Saxon, and Protestant, today things look and sound very different. People of color, language differences, minority cultures, and communities of many religious faiths make up the new reality. Of course, the country was always home to more differences than most people would admit, but now these strike us wherever we go. Just as large numbers of ethnic neighborhoods and restaurants have sprung up everywhere, so now the towns and cities across the landscape have synagogues, temples, mosques, and shrines along streets that once had only churches and cathedrals. It has become increasingly impossible—and undesirable—to live within one's own ethnic and religious enclave. As society has become increasingly pluralistic, so has the American family.

In a sense, many families are a microcosm of the larger society. Different ethnic backgrounds, different languages, different customs, and different faiths often come together in the same household. These homes are especially well placed to prepare children for the diverse world they will enter. The question is, how can they best meet this challenge?

Before you can accomplish something worthwhile, you need to get a picture in your mind of what it is you want to accomplish. In the face of all the current diversity, many interfaith parents, not to mention educators, community leaders, and policy-makers, feel paralyzed. Not too many thinking people want to go back to the time when differences between people kept them apart and suspicious of each other. This kind of separation has led to cruel stereotyping, oppression, culture wars, and even ethnic cleansing. And yet, many people have a tradition and a faith they want to pass on to their children. It is something that has sustained them, called for their commitment, and provided a community of fellow pilgrims holding the same beliefs and hopes. Caught between wanting to embrace the pluralism of the world and yet maintaining one's own particular tradition makes it seem like a choice has to be made for one or the other. That is not necessarily the case, however. It is possible to find a way to bring your child up with a firm grounding in one faith while developing her appreciation and openness to the different faiths of others. Think of this latter task as having two main thrusts:

- *Show how it is done.*
  Some of the most permanent lessons a child will learn will be by watching you. How do you handle the differences between you and your partner? Do you support each other's faith journeys although you do not travel the same path? Do you not only allow your partner the freedom to be different but actually show an interest in his faith? Do you cooperate with his schedule of religious practices and attendances at services? Do you give him the space and time to practice his faith at home? Do you share together your struggles in belief and commitment in a mutually supportive way? Do you stay

attuned to the insights your partner's faith might have to offer you? Do you tell him what inspires you and gives you daily courage in the face of difficulty? Do you open your home to members of both religious communities? Are you willing to accompany him on special occasions? Do you minimize the impact of your differences from him as you arrange your daily schedules? Do you show respect for both faiths?

• *Teach how it is done.*

Even though you and your partner may have created a positive environment in which you all can flourish together despite your differences, there is still a need for teaching. Set against a background of behaviors and attitudes that accept and value differences, any lessons you teach your child by words will have the ring of conviction. This instruction can clarify and reinforce what you have endeavored to demonstrate. Do you answer your child's questions about your partner's faith without sounding critical or judgmental? Have you explained to her why you and she are going to services and your partner isn't joining you? Have you expected her to show the same respect for your partner's faith as you show? Have you allowed her to discover things about your partner's faith? Have you allowed your partner to talk about his faith to her? Have you given her the opportunity to get to know other children and adults from your partner's community? Have you involved your partner in ways he is comfortable with to help you teach her about your faith?

The faith (or faiths) you have chosen to share with your child does not ever have to be exclusionary or hostile to other faiths. Always look for opportunities to build bridges between you and different others, not to give your child a confused mish-mash of conflicting religious beliefs and ideas but to help her understand and appreciate the plurality that makes up the world of faith today. In meeting other faiths, her own can be strengthened through mutual support.

QUESTIONS AND ANSWERS

Is there any religious organization that encourages interfaith marriages?

It is impossible to speak for all faiths; but it can at least be said that few religious denominations actively encourage interfaith marriages. There are some communities, however, that may be more hospitable to an interfaith family. These are usually the more liberal congregations of particular religions. Some religious groups are founded on egalitarian principles, such as Unitarian Universalism, and are purposefully open to many faiths.

What makes some religions more compatible than others?

The greater the common ground shared between faiths the more likely it is that they will be compatible. This common ground may be comprised of shared beliefs. An Episcopalian and a Roman Catholic may be more compatible than an Episcopalian and a Buddhist, for instance. Shared histories also bring a measure of compatibility. Protestants of all denominations and Catholics may be more comfortable together than with Jews or Taoists. Monotheists, such as Jews, Christians, and Muslims, may find more in common among themselves than with polytheists such as Hindus, or atheists, although

other differences among monotheists are often just as insurmountable. Perhaps the most significant compatibility factors
have less to do with beliefs and more to do with other considerations. Culture is a big factor. All religions are shaped as
much by cultural conditions as they are by dogma and practice. Hinduism and Buddhism are more beyond the reach of
westerners because of their Indian and Asian roots and ways
of thinking. Islam is a cultural world apart from Christianity
and even Judaism to some extent. The other major factor is
the level of fundamentalism to which the religion subscribes.
Fundamentalist religions are usually authoritarian and pro-
hibit any deviation from prescribed religious practices and beliefs. A fundamentalist partner, by this definition, would be less
able to compromise and negotiate a consensus with a non-
believing partner. He or she would, however, be less likely to
marry outside of the faith.

**Does marrying somebody outside of my faith indicate
that my faith is not important to me?**

This is a common assumption and sometimes true. There
is a certain logic to saying that if you cared about your faith,
you would want to raise your child in that faith, without putting that at risk if your partner does not agree with you. Further, since faith is a way of life, it is threatened when you have
to negotiate with a non-believing partner how you both shall
live together. However, in too many cases, this logic breaks
down. Your partner may recognize that your faith is important
enough to you that you both will work together to raise your
child in it. Negotiating with a partner on how you will live does
not necessarily weaken faith; it may actually strengthen it. For
one thing, it makes you think about what is important to you
and prompts you to prioritize your values. For another, it may
result in a richer, broader environment in which a particular

faith can grow. In other words, all your actions, choices, and learnings together determine the level of importance of your faith, not a single (albeit significant) decision.

Should all the children in a family be raised in the same faith?

Some interfaith families choose to raise their children in different faiths so that both parents have the responsibility and privilege of passing their religious heritage on to at least one of their children. An advantage of this approach is that it may relieve tensions between parents who find other alternatives to handling their religious differences unacceptable. It can also maximize the opportunities for learning how to appreciate different others as brothers and sisters learn about their respective faiths from each other. A disadvantage to this arrangement is that rivalry might set in between different members of the family. Parents would need to guard against favoring one child over another. Such a plan does not solve all the problems of an interfaith marriage, because negotiations would still be needed over which festivals and holy times would be celebrated by the family, how different schedules could be juggled, and what give and take is needed in a host of other family matters to keep both sides satisfied that their religious needs were being met.

What about changing the child's religious upbringing at some point?

When both parents want to expose their child to their religious faith but realize the difficulties of doing this simultaneously, they might consider raising him through his elementary school years in one faith. Then later on, say when he changes schools, he also changes religion. Such a plan carries with it many of the same kinds of advantages and disadvantages as bringing him up in both religions all along. There would still be the possibility of confusing him with conflicting claims, of overwhelming him with too much religion, and of confronting him with the likelihood of ultimately having to make a choice that will favor one parent over the other. It would, however, lessen the immediate pressures on him of trying to maintain two sets of beliefs and practices at the same time, while giving both parents the opportunity to share their faith with him. Of course, there is the distinct possibility that when it comes time to change religious direction, it may appear to you all that this would be too disruptive to his religious, as well as social, life. Again, this is an option that need not be excluded from consideration, but should be weighed carefully. Generally, however, this choice makes for a very bumpy ride.

GLOSSARY

All Saints' Day a Christian celebration on November 1 commemorating all those who are thought to reside in heaven. Many Protestant groups reject the notion and the day.

Apocrypha a collection of books not included in the original Hebrew Bible but added by some Christian churches, including Roman Catholic and Greek and Russian Orthodox. These books are usually not accepted by Protestant groups.

Ash Wednesday the first day of Lent (the forty-day period before Easter). It is signalled by having ashes marked on the forehead of priests or members. Celebrated by Roman Catholics, Anglicans, and some Protestant churches.

Baptism Christian initiation service in which converts are immersed in water or water is sprinkled over them.

Bar Mitzvah/Bat Mitzvah Jewish religious coming-of-age ceremony for boys at thirteen and girls at twelve or thirteen, when they are considered old enough to participate in all the Jewish rituals. Usually involves a festive feast with family and friends.

Bhagavad Gita poetic text in honor of the Hindu god Krishna.

Bible the Christian canon of sacred writings. Usually includes the 39 books of the Old Testament and the 27 books of the New Testament. Derived from the Latin word for "books."

Bodhi Tree   the tree of awakening; the fig tree under which Buddha sat waiting for enlightenment.

Buddhism   one of the world's major religions, founded by Siddhartha Gautama (566–486 B.C.E.), who became known as the Buddha. Spread through India and much of Asia and more recently to Europe and North America. Among its key teachings are that suffering is a part of existence; that desire is the principal cause of suffering; that by discipline one can overcome desire, and that one is rewarded ultimately with *nirvana.*

Catechism   a manual of instruction used to teach about Christianity.

Charismatic   a descriptor used to identify those religious groups that focus on the role of the Holy Spirit in Christian life. The presence of the Spirit is attained through baptism and demonstrated through speaking in tongues, healings, and other spiritual gifts. From the Greek *charisma* meaning gift or favor.

Christianity   the largest of the world's religions. Accepts Jesus Christ as the founder and object of worship, believing him to be the *Messiah* promised in Jewish history. Arose in Palestine and the Mediterranean region in the first century C.E. Among its key teachings are that human beings are alienated from God; that Jesus is both human and divine; and that Jesus' life, teachings, death by crucifixion, and resurrection heals the relationship between God and humankind.

Christmas   Christian feast on December 25 celebrating the birth of Jesus.

Church building for public Christian worship.

Communion see Eucharist.

Confucianism East Asian faith traditions built on the thought of Confucius, known as the First Teacher. Focuses on the ultimate values of human life by asking, "What makes life worth living?" and, "What virtues and methods of self-discipline will create a worthy human civilization?"

Congregation a community held together by religious bonds.

Crucifix a representation of the cross on which Jesus died.

Crucifixion method of execution involving tying or nailing a person to a cross. The death of Jesus.

Doctrine systematic beliefs of a religious tradition.

Easter Christian celebration recalling the death and resurrection of Jesus. It is a high point in the church year. The predecessor of this celebration is the Jewish Passover.

Ecumenism the search for understanding among the various Christian denominations and world religions through dialogue and collaboration.

Eightfold Path of Buddhism the path taken to end suffering and the desire that prompts it. Includes right belief; right resolve; right speech; right behavior; right occupation; right effort; right contemplation; right concentration.

Enlightenment coming to know the nature and causes of suffering, as understood in the Buddhist tradition. Siddhartha Gautama, the Buddha, is thought to have reached this state as he sat under the Bodhi Tree. In some sects, it is believed that many others have and can reach this state.

Eucharist the most significant Christian ritual involving a ceremony with bread and wine that commemorates the death and resurrection of Christ. In various Christian communities it is also known as Communion, Last Supper, or Mass. Its roots are traced back to the last supper of Jesus before his death in which he offered the usual blessing of food and drink to point to the significance of his imminent death. A major point of departure of Protestants from Catholics is that the latter believe the bread and wine to be actually transformed into the body and blood of Christ, where the former take them as symbols representing the body and blood of Christ.

Faith tradition/Faith community a group who share a common set of moral, spiritual, or religious truths.

Five Pillars of Islam the five duties of true believers in the Islamic faith are to recite the creed, "There is no God but Allah, and Mohammed is his Prophet;" worship one God and pray to him at least three times a day; practice charity and help the needy; fast in the month of Ramadan; and make a pilgrimage to Mecca at least once in a lifetime, if possible.

Fundamentalism the looking back to historic roots and models of faith and a rejection of modern trends that would in any sense "water down" the faith. Fundamentalists exist in most faiths.

God the infinite and eternal Being. In less traditional faith systems, "God" may refer to whatever is regarded as the ultimate source of goodness and meaning. Recognized by many religions as the Creator, Sustainer, and Judge of the world. *Monotheism*—belief in one God (including the Christian view of a three-person Godhead of Father, Son, and Holy Spirit). *Polytheism*—belief in many gods. *Atheism*—opposition to belief in God. *Agnosticism*—denying all possibility of knowledge of God. Derived from the Anglo-Saxon word for "good."

Good Friday   holy day celebrated on the Friday of the Christian Holy Week before Easter. In Christian belief, Jesus was crucified and died on Friday.

Gospel   the announcement and story of the birth, life, and death of Jesus and the salvation Christians believe this brings. From the Greek word for "good news."

Gospels   the first four books of the New Testament that recount Jesus' life.

Guru   a Hindu spiritual mentor, teacher, or leader.

Hanukkah   Jewish festival usually falling in December that celebrates freedom in memory of a victory in the 2nd century B.C.E. For eight days, a candle is lit on one of the branches of an eight-branched candlestick (menorah). Gifts are exchanged and special foods are eaten. Also spelled Chanukkah.

Hashem   the Hebrew word for God.

Heaven   the home of God. A place of beauty, life, worship, and glory, or a state of bliss.

Hell   the final abode of everlasting torment for the damned, according to Christian doctrine.

Hinduism   a major world religion, most commonly found in India but with believers throughout the world. Although it has no fixed creed it does have some beliefs more or less in common, including the view that the world has always existed although constantly undergoing transformations or cycles of change; Brahman is the world-soul or universal essence; human beings are part of the world-soul and so their souls live forever even though the body may die; and that human duty is to be in harmony with the soul.

Holy consecrated, sacred, morally and spiritually perfect; devoted to God or the worship of God.

Immaculate Conception the belief that Mary, the mother of Jesus, was from conception free of any trace of sinfulness. This belief is one that separates Catholic doctrine from Protestant.

Islam a major world religion with roots in Arab lands. Arabic term means "submission" to the one God, Allah. Accepts seventh-century C.E. prophet Muhammad as the last and final messenger of God; it is the youngest of the major world religions.

Jainism an Indian religion founded in the sixth century B.C.E. Major beliefs are similar to Hinduism, and include the ideas that a human being is the product of soul-substance mixed with the consequences of good and bad deeds (karma) in a cycle of rebirths; liberation from the cycle of rebirths is brought about by reducing bad karma through discipline and knowledge; and supports the belief that no life form should be injured physically, psychologically, or intellectually.

Judaism a major world religion from which Christianity and Islam later arose. Accepts the Five Books of Moses, *Torah*, as the foundation of God's revelation to humankind. Includes belief in one God as Creator and Judge; human beings have free will and must choose between good and evil; justice and truth are primary virtues because God is just and true; the Ten Commandments were given by God as a guide and law for all.

Kosher   Jewish dietary rules about what should and should not be eaten and how foods should be stored and prepared; also a way of life.

Last Supper   see *Eucharist.*

Lent   a forty-day period preceding Easter, during which forms of penance and fasting are undertaken in commemoration of the sacrifice of Jesus.

Liturgy   a ritual of public worship, usually well established and often printed for members to follow and participate in.

Mantra   usually a sequence of sounds used as a meditational device in Hinduism, Buddhism, and Jainism.

Mary, Mother of God   the mother of Jesus, a Jewish peasant woman. Roman Catholics, in contrast to Protestant Christians, venerate her, having developed the doctrine that she was born and lived without a trace of sinfulness and is now in heaven where she protects and nurtures believers. Various appearances of Mary, "Marion Apparitions," have been reported and become regarded as sites for special prayers and healings. Also known as the Blessed Virgin Mary.

Mass   the Catholic Eucharistic ritual in which bread and wine serve as the body and blood of Christ. The Mass has its own order, which includes a greeting from the presider, an opening prayer, a hymn of praise, Old and New Testament readings with a psalm response, an allelujah refrain, a reading from the Gospels, recitation of the creed, intercessory prayers, preparation of the altar and gifts, prayer of thanksgiving, consecration of the bread and wine, the Lord's prayer, a sign of peace among the members, taking the bread and wine, and a concluding blessing. This outline is also similar to that followed by Orthodox and Anglican liturgies. See *Eucharist*.

Meditation   contemplation, often in a formal way, especially among Buddhists, Hindus, and Taoists where it serves to bring tranquility and insight.

Middle Way   the life espoused by the Buddha from the time of his first sermon. A balanced life, avoiding the extremes of self-denial and self-indulgence.

Minister   preacher or pastor in many Christian churches.

Mosque   place of worship for Muslims.

Nativity   literally, birth. In the Christian context, it refers particularly to the birth of Jesus. A typical nativity scene or reenactment includes the manger or feed trough which served as a cradle, Mary and Joseph as Jesus' earthly parents, cows and sheep around the stable, and shepherds and wise men as visitors. The star that guided the wise men to the right place and a choir of angels may also be represented.

New Testament   collection of materials written by early Christians and later canonized into scripture.

Nirvana   the ultimate end sought by Hindus and Buddhists. It represents the end of repeated rebirths and suffering. For Hindus, this means absorption into universal spirit. For Buddhists, it means ultimate awakening, and in some cases, something more but indescribable.

Old Testament Christian name for the books of the Hebrew Bible that have been adopted as part of the Christian Bible.

Pagan a once-derogatory term for someone not religious but now being rehabilitated to refer to newly revived primitive or nature religions.

Passover eight-day Jewish holiday remembering the rescue of the Hebrews from Egypt when the angel of death "passed over" the homes of believers, protecting their firstborn from death. Celebrated with a traditional seder meal.

Penance the penalty for violating a religious law.

Priest leader in religious rituals or a religious teacher. In Catholicism, the priest is celibate.

Protestantism Christian religious groups that rose out of controversies and doctrinal differences with the Roman Catholic Church since the beginning of the Reformation in the sixteenth-century C.E. There are more than two thousand Protestant groups today.

Purim Jewish holiday commemorating the deliverance of Jews from Persia as told in the Book of Esther. It is a time for dressing up in costumes, parties, exchanging delicacies, and retelling the story of Esther.

Qur'an the scriptures of Muslims. Also known as Koran.

Rabbi intellectual and spiritual leader of the Jewish community.

Ramadan month in which Muslims engage in daytime fast.

Reformation a movement to reform Christian beliefs and practices in the sixteenth and seventeenth centuries that produced a number of Protestant denominations deeply divided from the Roman Catholic Church.

Reincarnation   belief in the rebirth of the soul in successive life forms.

Religion   system of beliefs and practices that relate to God or whatever is taken to be ultimate.

Rosary   a string of beads used to count repeated prayers.

Rosh Hashanah   along with Yom Kippur, the holiday that makes up the High Holidays (Days of Awe) of the Jewish calendar. In late September or October, Rosh Hashanah is marked by the blowing of the *shofar,* or ram's horn, as a call to repentance.

Sacrament   a ritual, believed to have been instituted by Christ, which gives a sense of and imparts the presence and grace of God. Among the sacraments are the Eucharist, Baptism, Matrimony, and Anointing the Sick.

Sacred   persons, places, or things set apart for their spiritual significance.

Scriptures   holy books.

Secular   concerned with this world, worldly; not sacred.

Shintoism   a Japanese religion. Beliefs usually include great respect for the natural world and ancestors; royalty can take on divine status; the social group rather than the individual is the important consideration; an emphasis on local cults rather than national religion means that Shintoism is seen in many forms.

Siddhartha Gautama   personal name of the Buddha, the young prince who set out to seek enlightenment and became the founder of Buddhism. Believed by some to be the final incarnation of the one who sought enlightenment. Literally, "he whose aims are fulfilled."

Spirituality   concerned with the sacred, the holy, and life-meanings beyond the surface appearance of the material world.

Stations of the Cross   fourteen depictions of events in the last days of Jesus' life usually arranged along the walls of Catholic churches.

Synagogue   a Jewish place of worship and communal center.

Talmud   collection of explanations and clarifications of the Jewish code, or laws.

Taoism   a Chinese religion primarily concerned with spiritual transformation of people and societies by freeing them from mundane concerns to live in harmony with deeper, abiding realities. Taoist beliefs emphasize individual, social, and political reintegration with cosmic forces, known as the Tao.

Temple   building set apart for the presence of God or for worship.

Theist   one who believes in the existence of God or gods.

Theology   doctrine or study of God or gods.

Torah   God's revelation to Moses on Mount Sinai. The five books of Moses, or in common usage, the whole Hebrew Scriptures.

Vishnu   Hindu god believed to be the protector of the universe. Usually depicted in multi-armed human form.

Worship   reverence and adoration given to God. May be as a formal service or an informal devotion.

Yarmulke   skullcap worn by Jewish men and now sometimes women in prayer and religious ceremonies to show reverence for God. Orthodox Jews may wear the skullcap all the time.

Yom Kippur   Day of Atonement, the most solemn day in the Jewish calendar, when prayers are made for the forgiveness of sins and for a good life for the coming year. Coming ten days after Rosh Hashanah, it occurs in late September or October. The service begins with the chanting of Kol Nidre, a favorite prayer, and ends with Ne'illah, a service of "closing of the gates," once symbolizing those of Jerusalem, now the end of the day of prayer, fasting, and penitence.

SUGGESTED READINGS AND RESOURCES

Arnstein, Helene. *Between Mother-In-Law and Daughter-In-Law.* New York: Dodd, Mead & Co., 1985. (Suggests ways of strengthening the significant relationship between mothers-in-law and daughters-in-law.)

Boadt, Lawrence, Helga Croner, and Leon Klenicki, eds. *Biblical Studies: Meeting Ground of Jews and Christians,* New York: Paulist Press, 1980. (Explores the common theological ground of the Jewish and Christian traditions.)

Charlesworth, James H. *Overcoming Fear Between Christians and Jews.* Philadelphia: American Interfaith Institute; New York: Crossroad, 1992. (Explains the beliefs and practices of Jews and Christians to make them accessible to the other.)

Cowan, Paul, and Rachel Cowan. *Mixed Blessings: Marriage Between Jews and Christians.* New York: Doubleday, 1987. (Written by a Jewish couple from different religious roots, this book offers advice to Jewish-Christian families based on their findings and research in working with many interfaith couples.)

Crohn, Joel. *Mixed Matches: How To Create Successful Interracial, Interethnic, and Interfaith Relationships.* New York: Fawcett Columbine, 1995. (One of the few reference books that goes beyond Jewish-Christian relationships, the book gives many personal accounts and advice for making interfaith and intercultural homes work.)

Eck, Diana L. *Encountering God.* Boston: Beacon Press, 1993. (Recounts a scholar's personal confrontation with and study of a faith—Hinduism—altogether different from her own—Methodism—and what she has learned from the experience.)

Gertz, Susan Enid. *Hanukkah and Christmas at My House.* Middletown, Ohio: Willow and Laurel Press, 1991. (A children's book to help them understand and appreciate both the Christian and Jewish traditions they inherit.)

Goodman-Malamuth, Leslie, and Robin Margolis. *Between Two Worlds: Choices for Grown Children of Jewish-Christian Parents.* New York: Simon and Schuster, 1992. (Examines the personal and communal impact on the grown children from interfaith families from the perspective of the authors' own experiences and research.)

Gottlieb, Beatrice. *The Family in the Western World.* New York: Oxford University Press, 1993. (Traces the dynamics of family life from medieval times to the present.)

Gruzen, Lee. *Raising Your Jewish/Christian Child: Wise Choices for Interfaith Parents.* New York: Dodd, Mead, and Co., 1987. (Endorses the possible benefits of Jewish-Christian homes and gives practical suggestions on and illustrations of how to achieve good results.)

Hawxhurst, Joan. *Bubbe and Gram: My Two Grandmothers.* Kalamazoo, MI: Dovetail, 1996. (Reclaims children's dual heritage in growing up with Jewish and Christian roots.)

Hawxhurst, Joan. *Interfaith Wedding Ceremonies: Samples and Sources.* Kalamazoo, MI: Dovetail Publications, 1996. (Gives sample wedding services for Jewish and Christian marriages officiated respectively by a priest, minister, and judge, and various combinations with a rabbi or Jewish scholar, plus helpful advice on planning for the wedding.)

Hick, John. *God Has Many Names* Philadelphia: Westminster Press, 1980. (A study on the nature of religion and religious belief that illustrates how much religions actually have in common.)

King, Andrea. *If I'm Jewish and You're Christian, What Are the Kids? A Parenting Guide for Interfaith Families* New York:

UAHC Press, 1993. (Offers guidance to Jewish-Christian families for dealing with children and their own relationship through all the cycles of life from babyhood to old age.)

Mahmoody, Betty. *Not Without My Daughter.* New York: St. Martin's Press, 1987. (Tells the story of one American woman's harrowing experience getting herself and her daughter out of Iran after her husband's rededication to the Shi'ite Muslim faith.)

McElrath, William N. *Ways We Worship.* Hauppauge, NY: Barron's Educational Series, Inc., 1997. (A book for children that describes key elements in the world's faiths.)

Petsonk, Judy, and Jim Remsen. *The Intermarriage Handbook: A Guide for Jews and Christians.* New York: William Morrow, 1988. (Offers practical tips, research, and case studies for families dealing with the religious, emotional, and psychological effects of marriage between Jews and Christians.)

Rosenbaum, Mary Helene Pottker, and Stanley Ned Rosenbaum. *Celebrating Our Differences: Living Two Faiths in One Marriage.* Shippensburg, PA: White Mane Publishing Co., Inc., 1994. (Gives practical advice on maintaining one's faith in an interfaith family and raising children with the benefits of parents of different faiths.)

Yob, Iris M. *Keys to Teaching Children About God.* Hauppauge, NY: Barron's Educational Series, Inc., 1996. (Outlines approaches to the religious upbringing of children that is responsive to a multifaith world.)

Magazines that you might consider:
Interrace, P. O. Box 12048, Atlanta, GA 30355
Dovetail, P. O. Box 19945, Kalamazoo, MI 49019

These web sites may also be helpful:
Wedding Central: http://www.weddingcentral.com For information about intercultural wedding customs, look under "Wedding Traditions and Customs."
Interfaith Marriages Inc: http://www.interfaith.org/referrals/

INDEX